JUMP FOR JOY!

Over 375 creative movement activities for young children

MYRA K. THOMPSON

PARKER PUBLISHING COMPANY
West Nyack, New York 10995

10 9 8 7 6 5 4 3 2 1

Library of Congress Cataloging in Publication Data

Thompson, Myra K.
    Jump for joy! : over 375 creative movement activities for young
children / Myra K. Thompson ; illustrated by Cherie A. Weaver.
        p.   cm.
    "Including simple directions for making your own inexpensive
equipment!"
    Includes bibliographical references and index.
    ISBN 0-13-512369-0
    1. Movement education—United States.   2. Activity programs in
education—United States.   I. Title.
GV452.T46   1993
372.86—dc20   92-23923
                                                                              CIP

ISBN 0-13-512369-0

Parker Publishing Company
Business Information Publishing Division
West Nyack, NY 10995

Simon & Schuster. A Paramount Communications Company

Printed in the United States of America

About the Author

Myra Thompson received her Bachelor of Arts in Physical Education from the University of Northern Iowa. As a Peace Corps Volunteer, Myra worked to develop elementary physical education programs in Costa Rica. She taught elementary physical education at Marshalltown, Iowa Area Catholic Schools for nine years. Additionally, she has coordinated a number of YMCA youth programs. For the past four years she has been the movement specialist and the summer school-age program coordinator for Marshall County Child Care Services. She presents many workshops to preschool teachers and childcare personnel.

Myra has been an adjunct instructor in physical education at Marshalltown Community College and a GED instructor for Iowa Valley Community College District. She is a member of the state and national Association for the Education of Young Children, Kappa Delta Pi, and American Alliance for Health, Physical Education, Recreation, and Dance.

Myra's family consists of her husband Rich, their two children Ellen and Jeff, and their dog, Mike. They are all joyful movers.

About This Resource

JUMP FOR JOY! Over 375 Creative Movement Activities for Young Children will help you enhance the preschool and kindergarten curriculum with a wide variety of creative movement experiences. You do not need to have a background in movement to teach and enjoy the movement activities and games in this resource. All are written and illustrated to make it easy for you to lead young children in challenging, invigorating, and fun movement experiences.

All of these activities have been used successfully with children from age three to age five. By making occasional adaptations you should find them useful with younger and older children as well. The activities have been organized for easy use into fourteen sections. The first thirteen sections are labeled according to equipment requirements, while the fourteenth section provides activities for use with special holidays or seasons.

The sections are further divided into sixty lessons. Each lesson offers a range of activities that have been classroom-tested to flow easily from one into the other, starting with a warm-up, an equipment activity, or both, and continuing with individual, partner, and group activities. Equipment needs stay roughly the same within each lesson.

You can use the activities in the format offered or pick and choose from them as you wish. The equipment needed is basic, and many suggestions for constructing your own low-cost equipment or finding inexpensive sources are included. Some of the equipment you might be using are balls of various sizes (including old tennis balls), bean bags, hula hoops, scoops made out of milk jugs, buckets made out of ice cream containers, an easy-to-build balance beam, mats, flying disks, a homemade obstacle course, a parachute, ribbons you can easily make, and simple musical instruments you can buy or make. A number of activities require no equipment at all.

One of the goals of the movement education approach is to have all the children active and involved at the same time. That is important for a couple of reasons: there is less chance for embarrassment on the part of individual children, and because no one is waiting for a turn there are fewer discipline problems. The movement education approach also stresses children's creativity. Rather than telling and demonstrating exactly how to move, you pose each activity in terms of a challenge or problem to solve. For instance, you might ask, "Can you move backwards while staying low to the ground?" There is no one correct way for children to do this. They might crawl or slide, tummy up, tummy down, or on their side. Children are challenged to move creatively through open-ended questions. At the same time, they are thinking before moving—solving the problem of how to meet each challenge. They are also learning body and movement vocabulary, and exploring all the wonderful ways in which their bodies can move.

The games in this resource are generally cooperative, either organized so that no players are eliminated, or so that the children must work together in order to be successful. This eliminates all of the hurt feelings children used to have when they were eliminated in a game, and it ensures that everyone gets lots of movement practice. (Have you ever noticed that in a system of elimination, the very children who need the most practice are the ones least likely to get it?)

The introduction to Section 1, *Basic Movement Activities*, defines and details the basic sets of movement variables this resource will teach. While it is not necessary to learn them as such, you may find it useful to do so, especially if you want to develop any of your own activities. It is definitely recommended, however, that you teach the activities in Section 1 first, since they help both you and the students become familiar with movement terms and guidelines. After that the sections appear in no particular order and can be used as you wish. Lessons are given in roughly sequential form, but that does not mean you cannot use activities from them as you see fit.

You don't need to be a professional physical educator or a superior athlete with the ability to demonstrate myriad physical activities to lead these activities. You simply present the material by asking questions, which this resource provides, and the children take over from there. You will only need to supervise their activities, be enthusiastic, and try to keep up with all of the cries of "Hey, look at me!"

It is important that you participate with the children. Young children are great mimics, and if you just stand around and watch they will tend to do the same. Constantly move about the room, praising the children and pointing out all of the great things you are seeing. Enthusiasm is contagious. Keep in mind two key words: *jump*—this resource should be a jumping-off point, a source of stimulation and inspiration to provide an endless variety of creative movement experiences; and *joy*—keep the movement experience joyful!

Myra K. Thompson

Contents

Basic Movement Lessons

INTRODUCTION

This series of lessons introduces basic movements and serves as a base for the great variety of activities that follow. For your reference, here is a brief discussion of those basic movements and movement variables.

Large motor movements are of two types, *locomotor movements* and *non-locomotor movements*. Locomotor movements are the traveling movements. They carry the body from one place to another. The basic locomotor movements are:

Walking: Stepping from one foot to the other in even rhythm.

Running: Stepping from one foot to the other in a fast, even rhythm. Both feet are momentarily off the ground at the same time.

Hopping: Springing from one foot and landing on the same foot in an even rhythm.

Jumping: Springing from one or two feet and landing on two feet in an even rhythm.

Leaping: Taking off from one foot with a spring and landing on the opposite foot in an even rhythm. The body is momentarily suspended in the air, with the rear leg extended backward in the air and the front leg extended forward for the landing.

Skipping: Stepping on one foot and hopping on the *same* foot, then stepping on the opposite foot and hopping on that foot in an uneven rhythm.

Galloping: Moving forward with the same foot always in front. A step followed by a quick close of the other foot on the uneven beat.

Sliding: A sideways gallop. A step on one foot and a quick close of the other foot up to the first on the uneven beat.

Non-locomotor movements are movements that do not carry the whole body from one place to another. These movements are performed from a relatively stable base of support, such as standing, kneeling, or lying down. Examples of non-locomotor movements are: swinging and swaying; bending and stretching; twisting; and reaching and recoiling. Reaching, of course, is a movement of any body part away from the body. Recoiling is bringing the body part back in toward the body. These movements can be light or strong, fast or slow.

Another class of movements is that of *manipulative movements*. These movements involve the handling of objects. Throwing and catching are examples of basic manipulative movements.

We can move using both locomotor and non-locomotor movements according to a number of *movement variables*. The following movement variables are the ones stressed in this book. As you become familiar with them you will discover that they can be used alone or in any combination. The use of these variables accounts for an infinite number of movements challenges. Don't just use the movement variables, but teach them to the children. Not only will they develop a wonderful movement vocabulary, but they will also grasp some very basic movement concepts.

The movement variables are:

- Moving in different directions
  —forward
  —backward
  —sideways (left and right)
- Moving at different levels
  —*high level* is the space above one's shoulders.
  —*medium level* is the space between one's shoulders and knees.
  —*low level* is the space below one's knees.
- Moving in different pathways
  —straight
  —curved
  —zigzag
- Body shapes
  —round
  —straight and narrow
  —straight and wide
  —twisted

The diagram on the next page may be of some help in remembering the movement variables. Why not make large posters for the room?

There are two basic movement education terms used to describe our use of space. *Self-space* is the space our own body uses at any given time. An easy way for preschoolers (or anyone else) to understand the term is that self-space is "the

Movement Variables

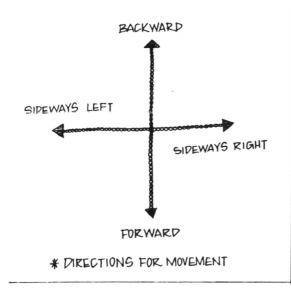

BACKWARD

SIDEWAYS LEFT

SIDEWAYS RIGHT

FORWARD

✱ DIRECTIONS FOR MOVEMENT

HIGH

MEDIUM

LOW

✱ LEVELS FOR MOVEMENT

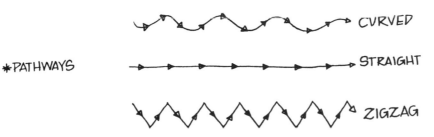

✱PATHWAYS

CURVED

STRAIGHT

ZIGZAG

STRAIGHT
AND NARROW

ROUND

STRAIGHT
AND WIDE

TWISTED

✱SHAPES

space I use by myself." General space is the space everyone uses together. It might be a classroom, a gymnasium, or an area of the playground. Maybe an easier term for preschoolers would be "everybody space," the space everybody uses together.

LESSON 1

Body Stretches (Warm-up)

Equipment: None.

The children are in a scattered formation.

1. *Reach up high with your hands and stretch up tall on your tiptoes.*
2. *Stand tall with your arms overhead. Lean to the left, feeling your side stretch. Lean to the right and stretch.*
3. *Hold your arms straight out to the sides, shoulder-high, and reach your arms as far behind you as you can. Do you feel the stretch in your chest?*
4. *Sit down, with your legs straight out in front of you. Reach your hands as far forward as you can.*
5. *Keep sitting and fold your legs in front of yourself. Bend forward at the waist and reach forward with your arms.*

Space Exploration (Individuals)

Equipment: None. Cutout bleach bottle scoops (see Scoops and Tennis Balls, Section 4) worn as space helmets are optional.

The children are in scattered formation. *Today we are going to be space explorers. Reach your arms all around—to the sides, up high, behind you, twist and reach. The space your own body uses all by itself is called* self-space. *That makes sense doesn't it? The space I use by myself is my self space.*

1. Can you be very tall in your self space?
2. Very small?
3. Very wide? What does wide mean?
4. Very narrow? What does narrow mean?
5. Can you be very round in your self space?
6. Very twisted? Don't get so twisted that you cannot get undone!

Do you see all the different shapes you can make with your body? What are the names of the shapes? What is the name of the space you use all by yourself?

Blast Off! (Individuals)

Equipment: None. The space helmets are optional.

Each of you gets to fly your own spaceship. You are going to leave your self space now and travel to a different kind of space. This new space is called everybody space. *Everybody space is the space everybody shares together.* Point out the boundaries of the space, whether they be the walls of the room or boundary markers outdoors. *What do you think you have to watch out for as you move in everybody space? That's right, you have to watch out for the walls and the other people.*

Explain your stopping signal before the children begin moving. It could be a bell, a whistle, a buzzer, a drum, or the words *stop* or *freeze*. *Move carefully now in everybody space. Explore all of the space.*

A common problem is to teach the children to move at random. For some inexplicable reason, the children naturally end up moving in a circle, usually a counterclockwise circle. Encourage the young explorers to move to the corners of the room, back to the middle, to another corner or to the side of the room, across the room diagonally (corner to corner), and so on. Really praise those who are moving everywhere and are not stuck in a circular orbit.

Can your spaceship only go forward? What other directions can it go? As the children move, point out the directions you see. As the young explorers hear you, they too will try the new directions. After the children have explored the space for a bit, stop and review the directions: forward, backwards, sideways. *Do any of you have a spaceship that can go up and down? Show me! So the directions we can move are: forward, backwards, sideways, up, and down.*

Follow That Moon Creature! (Partners)

Equipment: None. Space helmets are optional.

Assign partners. The partners sit together in a scattered formation. *Your spaceships have now landed on the moon. The taller person is the space explorer, and the shorter person is the moon creature. The moon creature will move everywhere in our everybody space, and her space explorer friend will follow her. The partners should frequently change jobs.*

Allow lots of time for free exploration. But, also use this activity to help the children become familiar with the names of the various locomotor movements. Suggest the different locomotor movements, and after the children have experimented with them, stop and talk about them. A frequent error will be not making a distinction between a hop and a jump. Point out that a hop is on one foot and a jump is on two feet. The children may not understand what you mean when you say slide. Tell them it is a sideways gallop and see how they respond.

Moving Together (Partners)

Equipment: None. Space helmets are optional.

The children may keep their partner from the previous activity or you may assign different partners. *The space explorer and the moon creature have now become friends. Hold hands with your new friend and move everywhere on the moon.*

You may also suggest various locomotor movements for the children to try. And don't forget to add the variable of moving in different directions. Challenge the partners to move sideways, backwards, or up and down together! The children will be able to handle two challenges at once:

1. *Can you take giant steps backwards? Don't let go of your partner!*
2. *Can you tiptoe sideways with your partner?*
3. *Who can jump backwards with their partner?*
4. *Can you jump sideways with your partner?*

Children, I Shrank the House! (Individuals)

Equipment: At least a dozen boundary markers. Bleach bottles, milk jugs, spot markers, or chairs can be used.

Use the boundary markers to mark a *large* square in the room. This first square should actually take up most of the room. The children are in a scattered formation inside the square. *Pretend this is your house. Your mother is a scientist, an inventor, and she's working on an experiment as you move about the house. But listen carefully as you move, because your scientist-mom has a lot of accidents. So whenever you hear her shout "explosion!" immediately stop moving and crouch down right where you are, covering your head with your arms.*

Each time there is an explosion, move the boundary markers inward, so the everybody space gets smaller. Then the scientist (you) has to admit, "Children, I shrank the house." *Move carefully now that the house is smaller. The challenge always is to move without touching anyone.* Repeat the activity several times, and with each explosion move the boundary markers in.

1. *If the everybody space is smaller, should you move faster or slower?*
2. *Should you move with big steps or small steps?*

(Some children will think they are smaller if they crawl on the floor. Show them that they actually use more floor space if they are crawling.) End the activity by returning the space to its original size after the last explosion. The children can then move in their favorite way of moving.

LESSON 2

Shapes (Warm-up)

Equipment: Pictures of the basic shapes: round, straight and narrow, straight and wide, twisted.

As the teacher holds up pictures of each of the shapes, the children try to make that shape with their bodies. Some additional challenges might be the following:

1. *Can you make lots of circles all at once? Use your arms, your fingers, your legs, and your mouth.*
2. *Can you be straight and narrow while standing up? How can you be taller?*
3. *Can you be straight and narrow while lying down?*
4. *Can you be wide?*
5. *How can you be wide and tall?*
6. *Can you make your body into a twisted shape?*
7. *Can you be twisted and low to the ground?*

High to Low (Individuals)

Equipment: None.

Talk about the fact that they just made lots of shapes. *Sometimes you made the shapes when you were tall and high; other times you made the shapes by being low to the ground. These different heights are called* levels. *Sometimes you can be in between the high and low level—this is called the medium level.* As you call out the level, the children quickly respond by putting as much of their body as possible into that level. Also:

1. *Put just your hands up high.*
2. *Can you put your feet up high?*
3. *Can you put your head into the medium level?*
4. *Can you put your feet into the medium level?*
5. *Put your hands into the low level.*

We can also move in everybody space with our bodies at different levels.

1. *Move in everybody space and stay at a low level.*
2. *Can you move backwards at the low level?*
3. *How can you move if your body is at the medium level?*
4. *Can you be at the medium level and go backwards?*

5. *How can you move at the high level?*

6. *Can you move sideways while at the high level?*

Alphabet Shapes (Partners)

Equipment: Alphabet cards of the following letters: *A, C, i, l, L, O, P, S, T, U, V, X,* and *Y.* Each set of partners needs a jump rope (or inner tube or rubber band rope).

As you hold up each alphabet card, the partners try to make that shape together. It is not necessary to call the shapes by their letter names.

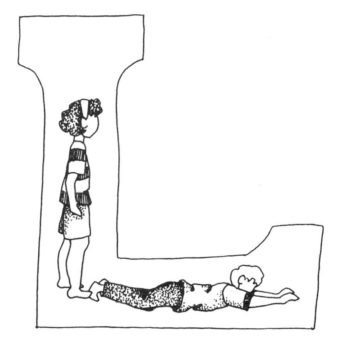

After the children have attempted to form all of the shapes with their bodies, give each pair a rope of some kind. As you hold up each card shape again, the children lay out that shape with their rope and then walk on the rope. *Remember to move backwards and sideways, too!*

Speedy Shapes (Partners)

Equipment: Shape and/or alphabet cue cards. Buzzer or bell is optional.

The children move freely about the room. When the children hear the signal "Speedy Shapes!" they are to quickly find a partner and make the shape indicated. You hold up a card showing the indicated shape as you give the verbal signal. The challenge is for the children to make the shapes as quickly as possible.

To add a further element of excitement, give the children a time limit, such as a slow count of five, for making the shapes. Sound an alarm or a buzzer when time is up. There need not be any consequence for those who don't finish on time.

Connected Shapes (Group)

Equipment: Tumbling mats are helpful, but not necessary.

This can be played by the total group, or it can first be done in smaller groups of four or five to make it easier. The children must all make the shape called out by the teacher. While they are all holding that shape, each person must also be touching someone else in the group.

1. *Make a twisted shape. Hold that shape and touch someone else in your group.*
2. *Can you only use your hands for touching someone else?*
3. *Can everyone be curved while touching someone else?*
4. *What happens if everyone is straight and narrow while touching someone else?*
5. *Let's try straight and wide.*

Have the children repeat all of the above challenges while standing, or being in the high level.

Fast Formations (Group)

Equipment: None.

Everyone moves freely in everybody space. When the teacher calls out a formation, the whole group responds as quickly as possible to make that formation.

1. *Form one circle.* Remind the children that the fastest way to make a circle is for each person to hold two people's hands.
2. *Line up one behind the other.*
3. *Line up side by side.*

This is a great activity for ending a movement session.

LESSON 3

I Can Draw With My . . . (Warm-up)

Equipment: Pictures of the various pathways: straight, curved, and zig-zag. Optional: alphabet cards that have those same shapes.

As the teacher holds up the picture of each shape, the children draw that shape in the air, first with one hand and then the other. Then have them try drawing the shapes with other body parts, such as the legs, the head, the hips, the elbows, and so on.

Point out that as you draw the curves the movement feels very smooth and soft. *How do the zigzags feel? Do they feel sharp, pointed, rough?*

Rambling Roads (Individuals)

Equipment: Plastic lids, spot markers, or other items to use as steering wheels—one per child. Gym tape to mark the floor is optional.

1. *Can you drive in a straight line? What will you do when you come to a wall?*
2. *Can you drive in a straight line backwards?*
3. *Can you drive as if you are going around a curve?*
4. *Can you curve one way and then the other? Do you lean into the curve?*
5. *Can you drive in a big curve? How about a little curve?*
6. *What happens if you keep going on the same curve? It becomes a circle!*
7. *Can you drive in a short, straight line and make a very sharp turn, then another straight line and a sharp turn, and keep going? This is called a zigzag. Keep your turns sharp!*
8. *Can you drive in curves going backwards?*

Partner Pathways (Partners)

Equipment: None. Gym tape to mark pathways on the floor is optional.

Assign partners. The partners move one behind the other, the back person holding onto the front person's waist or shoulders. Challenge the partners to move along the various pathways, going both forward and backward. Frequently change leaders.

Shape Tag (Group)

Equipment: Self-stick name tags—one per child. One third of the tags should have a drawing of a square on them; one third should have a drawing of a circle; and the other one third should have a drawing of a triangle. Also have one big drawing of each shape. Use gym tape or space markers to mark two lines at opposite ends of the room.

Put one name tag on the back of each child's hand. All of the children line up side by side on one line. The teacher stands in the middle of the playing area; she is the tagger. Call out the name of a shape. Any child wearing a tag with that shape must run to the line at the other end of the room. Any child tagged also becomes a tagger. The game is played until everyone is caught.

After every child has been tagged, have the children trade shape tags so everyone has a different shape. Play the game again.

The Shape Game (Group)

Equipment: Gym tape. Tape a large square, a large circle, and a large triangle onto the floor.

The children move freely about the room. When the teacher gives a stopping signal, each child must run to one of the shapes and stand inside it. The teacher then gives each shape a specific task. Examples: *Everyone in the circle jump up and down. Spin around if your are in the square. Clap your hands if you are in the triangle.*

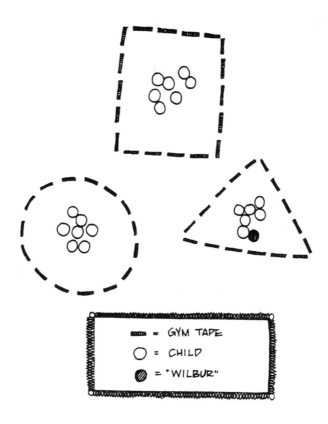

Variation: Make a big die out of a cardboard box. On two sides of the die draw a square, on two sides draw a circle, and on the other two sides draw a triangle. On the stopping signal the children go to a shape of their choosing and stand. You roll the die. Any children standing inside the shape that lands on top of the die must sit out one turn.

Where's Wilbur? (Group)

Equipment: Gym tape to mark a large circle, a large square, and a large triangle on the floor. One very tiny sticker is also needed.

The children move freely about the room. The teacher moves among the children and pretends to put a sticker on each child's back. When the teacher gives the stopping signal, everyone runs to a shape and stands inside it. The teacher then asks, "Where's Wilbur?" Wilbur is the person wearing the sticker. The children search among their friends inside their same shape, trying to find Wilbur. Wilbur then gets to decide how the children should next move. Play the game until everyone gets a chance to be Wilbur.

Large Ball Activities

INTRODUCTION

This series of lessons is designed for the use of 6-inch to 8½-inch *soft* rubber balls. The soft rubber balls available at local discount stores are actually more desirable for preschool use than are the rubber playground balls found in athletic supply catalogues. The "discount" balls are softer and lighter in weight, making them less threatening, safer, and easier to use.

The use of large balls will help the children to develop hand-eye and foot-eye coordination. It is important that the teacher encourage the children to use both the right and left sides of the body. The fact that the balls will be bouncing and rolling will challenge the students' sense of timing and their reflexes. And the balls will prove to be another resource for stimulating total body awareness.

Each lesson will include one or more:

- Equipment activities
- Warm-ups
- Individual challenges
- Partner challenges
- Group activities

Remember to review starting and stopping signals with the children before handing out the equipment. Based on the concept that "busy hands are happy hands," this series of lessons will always start with each child being given one ball.

The Equipment Activity that begins each lesson is designed to allow the children to begin moving immediately. Explain this activity before handing out the equipment. The children should begin with this task as soon as they get their ball.

LESSON 1

Sitting Toss and Catch (Equipment Activity)

Equipment: One ball per child.
Toss and catch the ball while sitting down.

Bouncing Bodies, Bouncing Balls (Warm-up)

Equipment: One ball per child.

Any lively music can be used. A particularly enjoyable selection for use with balls is "Bouncing Back to You" from the record *Aerobics for Kids*. The following is an example of a routine that can be done while holding on to the ball. Feel free to create your own movements and routines. Try to remember to alternate arm movements with leg movements. The focus should be on encouraging the children to mimic your actions rather than on doing each movement for a specific number of beats.

1. *Hold ball overhead and jump in place.*
2. *Stand in a wide stride. Make your arms go in a large circle, from above your head, around and down to your toes, and back up to your head.*
3. *Hold the ball on your tummy and jump.* The jump could be a jumping-jack jump, alternating from feet together to feet in a wide stride.
4. *Stand still and push the ball straight out from your tummy and pull it back close to your tummy.*
5. *Sit down. Hold the ball in your lap. Your legs are together and straight out in front of you. Bend your knees and bring your feet close in to your body. Then straighten your legs; then bend your knees bringing your feet in close.* Repeat several times.
6. *Exercise your arms! Move the ball over your head and then down to your tummy.* Repeat several times.
7. *March in place.*

Note: Five-year-olds will be challenged if you have them perform some arm and leg movements simultaneously.

Stop and Go Ball (Individuals)

Equipment: One ball per child.

1. *Hold the ball in your hands and walk in everybody space.* This allows the children to get used to moving with a ball while watching out for each other.

2. *Hold the ball and move other ways.* The children may explore freely and then the teacher may suggest specific movements: walk backwards, gallop, jog, hop, jump, slide sideways, etc.

3. *Toss the ball into the air and catch it.* You will have to challenge some children to toss higher and others to toss lower.

4. The children should move about the room while holding the ball. On a given signal, the children should stop, quickly toss the ball into the air and catch it. The signal might be a toot on a whistle, a bang on a tambourine, or a clap of the hands. Remember to vary the direction and type of movement.

5. *Bounce the ball and catch it.* Most children will be able to bounce and catch with success; others will be able to do a continuous dribble; and a few will be able to do a one-handed dribble.

Buddy Ball (Partners)

Equipment: One ball for every two people.

1. *You and your partner hold the ball between you with your tummies.*

2. *Keep holding the ball between your tummies and hold on to each other's hands. See if you can walk in the room without dropping the ball.*

3. *Try holding the ball back-to-back or front-to-back. Then see if you can move while holding the ball in this manner.*

Circle Ball (Group)

Equipment: One to ten balls.

Collect all of the balls and have the children make a sitting-down circle. Start with just one ball. Explain that you are now going to share the ball by passing it around the circle as quickly as possible.

After the ball has gone completely around the circle once, add this challenge: *When you get the ball this time, say your name loudly and then quickly pass the ball to the next person.*

The children will need to work on handing the ball to the next person, not tossing it. Explain that the person receiving the ball has to have her hands ready. *Keep your eyes on the person who will be giving you the ball!*

Continually challenge the group to go faster. As the children become comfortable with the activity, sneak additional balls into the circle. Then you will need to encourage the children to keep the balls moving and not to become collectors.

Blanketball (Group)

Equipment: One full-sized or queen-sized blanket for every ten to twelve children. One to ten balls for each blanket.

The children should be spaced evenly around the blanket, standing and holding onto the blanket.

Place one ball in the center of the blanket. Toss the ball into the air and try to catch it in the blanket. After a few attempts, stop the class and talk about the idea of tossing the ball lower so it is easier to catch. Place any number of balls on the blanket. The group should count to three together and give one big toss. Balls will fly everywhere, but see how many will come back down onto the blanket. (You may want to assign individuals to take turns retrieving the balls.) Keep tossing and catching that batch of balls until there are no balls left to catch. Then the retrievers should bring the balls back to the blanket and the game can start over.

For a less vigorous version of Blanketball, lay the blanket on the floor. (If the floor is tile, remind the children not to walk on the blanket: it will be slippery underfoot.) Have the children sit around the outside of the blanket. The children can roll a ball across the blanket to each other at random. The object is to keep the ball on the blanket. The game becomes more challenging as you add more balls.

LESSON 2

Toss and Catch in One Place (Equipment Activity)

Equipment: One ball per child.

Try to stay in your own space while you toss and catch the ball.

Fancy Feet (Warm-up)

Equipment: One ball per child. Music source is optional.

This activity may be done with music.

1. *Hold the ball in front of you and try to kick one foot up to touch the ball. Repeat this several times. Then try it with the other foot.*

2. *Stand with your feet in a wide stride position. Put the ball on the floor in front of one foot. Roll the ball back and forth from one foot to the other as fast as you can.*

3. *Hold the ball close to your tummy and hop. Be sure to take turns hopping on first one foot and then the other.*

4. *Stand with your feet together. Put the ball on the floor and roll it around your feet as fast as you can.*

5. Have them copy you by holding the ball high, or low, or to the left or right, or behind you while marching.

6. *Hold the ball in two hands and "draw" in the air with it. Make wavy lines, straight lines, curved lines, or zigzags.*

7. *Stand in a wide stride position with one foot in front and one foot in back. Hold the ball and jump, first with your left foot in front, then back, then front, then back.*

Penguin Shuffle (Individuals)

Equipment: One ball per child.

1. *Hold the ball between your feet and move.* Some children will move by jumping, and others will move by walking (which will look more like a waddling penguin.) *Remember, you can move in other directions, too. Try going backwards or sideways.*

2. *Hold the ball between your front flippers (elbows or upper arms) and move by tiptoeing. Try your favorite way of moving.*

3. *Put the ball on the floor and kick it. Remember to try first one foot and then the other.* If there is enough wall space, have the children kick the ball towards a wall. This will be an additional challenge, as they will need to stop the rebounding ball, either with their hands or their feet.

4. Repeat any of the activities from Lesson 1 or allow free exploration.

Friendly Ball (Partners)

Equipment: One ball for every two people.

1. *You and your partner sit down and roll the ball to each other.*

2. *Gently toss the ball to each other.* Talk about the fact that the two partners are close to each other so the toss should be soft. You may need to demonstrate an underhand toss.

3. *Stand up. If you have the ball, turn your back to your partner and roll the ball through your legs to your partner.* Explain that this is like hiking a football. Invariably both children will end up standing back-to-back, bent over, rolling the ball to each other. And that's okay, too!

4. *Find some other fancy way to get the ball to your partner.*

Circle Stride Ball (Group)

Equipment: One to four balls.

The children form a circle, then each person takes a small step backwards. The children should be standing with their feet in a wide stride, and their feet should be touching their neighbors' feet on either side of them.

The teacher stands in the middle of the circle. She may use any number of balls, but she should start with one while the children are learning the game. The children should stand with their hands on their knees. The teacher tries to roll the ball through the legs of any child, and that child uses his hands to stop the ball. If the ball goes through the legs of a child, that child chases the ball and brings it back to the circle.

As the children become more familiar with the game, three or four at a time may take the teacher's place in the middle. Have the children take two- or three-minute turns in the middle and then change players.

As the game is played the children tend to creep towards the center of the circle, so the circle is continually getting smaller. Frequently stop and have some or all of the children take a small step backwards in order to make room for everyone.

LESSON 3

Bounce and Catch (Equipment Activity)

Equipment: One ball per child.
Stay in your own space while you bounce and catch the ball.

Roads and Bridges (Warm-up)

Equipment: One ball per child.

1. *Sit down. Spread you feet wide apart. Put your ball right in front of you. With your fingers, gently roll the ball as far forward as possible. Keep your legs ("roads") straight and do not make any "bridges" under your "roads."*

2. *Now try to roll the ball on the floor all the way down one leg and then the other leg.* Encourage the children to go just as far as they can and to stop when their knee (or "bridge") comes off the ground. Repeat steps 1 and 2 several times.

3. *Hold the ball high above your head and gallop.*

4. *Stand still and hold the ball on your tummy. When I say "Up," raise the ball high above your head. When I say "Down," bring the ball back down to your tummy.* Repeat several times.

5. *Hold the ball behind your back and tiptoe backwards.*

6. *Hold the ball with your arms straight out in front of you. Now keep your feet still and twist your waist first to your left and then to your right.* (The actual directions are not important.) Repeat several times.

7. *Hold the ball and run in place.*

Elbows, Ears, Nose, and Toes (Individuals)

Equipment: One ball per child.

1. *Put the ball on the floor and stand next to it. As quickly as you can, touch each part of your body as I name it: ear, elbow, knee, toes, shoulder, etc.*
2. *Now as I name a part of your body, put that body part on the ball.* Only one part will be on the ball at one time. Remove the first part when the second part is called, and so on. When you ask the children to put a foot on the ball, remind them to just touch the ball lightly and not to stand on the ball. The children will soon be calling out body parts to use.
3. *Move about the room while holding the ball on the body part I call out.* Frequently change body parts called, as well as methods of movement.
4. *Try moving the ball on the floor using your hands. Then try your feet. Push the ball gently. Now try moving the ball with your elbow—your nose—your head!* Encourage the children to explore moving the ball with all the body parts they can think of.

Can You Use It? (Partners)

Equipment: One ball for every two people.

1. *Try to move the ball to your partner using a foot.*
2. Suggest other body parts that the children can use to get the ball to move between them.
3. Let the children explore and create. Some of the more skilled children may be able to stop the ball by using various body parts.

Body Ball (Group)

Equipment: One ball per child.

Each child should start with one ball; the ball should be on the floor with the child standing beside it. The children are to leave their ball on the floor and move about the room. When they hear the "Stop" signal, they are to go to the

closest ball and put their nose on it. You will need to practice this a couple of times, working with the children on going to the closest ball and not trying to find their "own" ball. Change the body part to be used each time. The game will be more of a challenge if you also change the method of movement each time.

It will be a real memory challenge if you tell the children the way to move and the body part to use *before* you say "Go." Do not repeat the body part when you say "Stop." Some children will devise their own memory aids, such as putting a hand on the special body part while they are moving.

To add yet another dimension to this activity, eliminate some balls while the children are moving. Tell the children ahead of time that you will be doing this and that they should *share* the balls. No one is eliminated! It is always a challenge to see how few balls you can end up with. If you add the element of music, this game becomes very much like the game **Sharing Musical Hoops**.

Helping Line (Group)

Equipment: One ball for each group of five to six children.

Divide the class into groups of five or six children. Have the children in each group line up one behind the other. Give the first child in each group a ball. Each child should pass the ball over his head to the person behind him. The last person in line then runs to the front of the line with the ball and starts the passing all over again.

This is a great game for ending a class. In this case, whoever is the last person in the line needs to take the ball, put it in the ball bag, and go sit by the door (or wait in an appropriate place). The children will need to pay close attention so they know when they are last. The teacher can keep starting new balls until each person has a chance to put away a ball.

LESSON 4

Foot to Foot (Equipment Activity)

Equipment: One ball per child.

Stand with your feet in a wide stride. Put the ball on the floor in front of one foot. Quickly roll the ball back and forth from one foot to the other.

Follow the Leader (Warm-up)

Equipment: One ball per child.

For the warm-up activity today we are going to pretend that the ball is leading you about the room. So if you have the ball in front of you, you will move forward. If you have the ball behind you, you will move backwards.

1. *Hold the ball in front of you and jog forward.*
2. *Hold the ball behind you and move backwards.*
3. *Hold the ball beside you and slide (gallop) sideways.*
4. *Now go sideways the other way. Remember to put the ball on the other side!*
5. *Hold the ball above your head, and jump up and down.*
6. *Hold the ball in front of you and move s-l-o-w-l-y.*
7. *Hold the ball beside you and jump sideways. Now try the other side.*
8. *You decide how to move, but let the ball lead the way.*

Pop Ups! (Individuals)

Equipment: One ball per child.

1. *Hold the ball in one hand and strike it off with your other hand.* You will need to demonstrate this, and you will need to talk about the word *strike.*

2. After the children have tried step 1 several times, have them try striking the ball with the other hand.

3. *Give the ball a little toss, and then strike the ball while it is in the air.*

4. *Toss the ball and try striking it with your other hand.*

5. *Can you hold the ball in your hand and strike it underneath?* You should demonstrate this. Ask the children what makes the ball go up.

6. *What would happen if you hit the top of the ball? Try hitting the ball very hard. Does it come back up very hard? Now try hitting the ball softly. Does it come back softly?*

7. Allow time for free exploration, frequently reminding the children to try using their other hand.

Partner Pop Ups (Partners)

Equipment: One ball for every two people.

1. The two partners should be a few feet away from each other, facing each other. *Put the ball on the floor and use your hand to hit the ball to your partner. The partner should catch the ball and lay it still before hitting it back.*

2. *Try it now using your other hand to strike the ball.*

3. *Can you turn your back to your partner and strike the ball so it goes through your legs to your partner?*

4. *Do you have to use just your hands to strike the ball? What other parts of your body can you use to get the ball to your partner?* Have the children show you their answers instead of telling you. Circulate about the room pointing out the great ideas you see.

5. *Try holding the ball in your hand and hitting it to your partner. We want to play safely. Do you think we should strike the ball hard or softly?*

6. *Can you strike the ball using your other hand?*

Clean Up, Pick Up, Tidy Up (Group)

Equipment: One to twenty balls, rubber band rope.

Divide the class into two groups. The groups should stand on opposite sides of a rubber band rope. The teacher can tie one end of the rope to a permanent fixture in the room and hold the other end herself. A responsible student could hold the other end of the rope, but it works best to have the teacher hold at least one end of the rope.

Each group starts with the same number of balls on their side of the rope. The balls can be placed on the floor in random fashion, or individuals may be assigned to hold the balls while you explain the game.

Explain that the Smith family children (indicate one group) are to clean up their backyard. They are to clean it up as quickly as possible by throwing all of the litter over the fence into the neighbor's yard. (At this point talk about the fact that you are just playing a game and you would not really do such a thing.) Then warn the children that they are absolutely not to go into the neighbor's yard because of the mean dog.

Likewise, the Ortega children (indicate the other group) on the other side of the fence are to clean up their own yard. And they must absolutely not cross over into the Smith family yard because of the ferocious cat.

Tell the children that when you give the stopping signal you will be looking for the children who are the fastest at sitting down with their hands in their laps. (Indeed, the hardest part of this game is stopping.) After the children play for a short while, stop the game and ask the children who did the best job of cleaning up their yard. You may need to explain that the family with the fewest number of balls really did the best job of getting rid of all of the litter in their yard.

Encourage the children to move quickly and get rid of one piece of litter at a time. (Some children will try to collect several balls and dump them over the fence all at once.) The game can be changed by having the children push the balls under the fence.

LESSON 5

Roll Around (Equipment Activity)

Equipment: One ball per child.

Sit down with the ball and try to roll it on the floor around yourself as fast as you can.

Aerobic-Ball (Warm-up)

Equipment: One ball per child, music source is optional.
This activity may be done with music.

1. *Hold the ball above your head. Bend your elbows and hold the ball behind your neck.* Alternately go up and down several times.

2. *Hold the ball on your tummy. Jump to the left and then to the right.* Repeat several times.
3. *Hold the ball to one side of your body and make circular motions. Now do it on the other side.* Repeat this two or three times.
4. *Lie on your back with your feet flat and your knees bent. Hold the ball on your tummy. Alternately raise one leg, straighten it, and lower your leg. Now raise your other leg, etc.* Repeat several times.
5. *Put one hand on either side of the ball. Push your hands together as hard as you can and hold. Take a short rest, then do it again.* Repeat several times.
6. *Hold the ball high, or low, or on the side. Try any fancy jump you like.*

Stop and Go Tosses (Individuals)

Equipment: One ball per child.

1. *Toss the ball and catch it. Now try tossing and catching while you are walking in the room.* Ask the children what two things they will have to watch for (other people and the ball). If they have to be watching for these two things, should they be tossing the ball really high?
2. *Try bouncing and catching the ball while moving about the room.*
3. *Try to toss or bounce the ball as you move in a different direction, backwards or sideways.*

Buddy Bounces (Partners)

Equipment: One ball per child.
Start with just one ball for two people. Then give each couple a second ball.

1. *Toss and catch the ball with your partner.*
2. *You and your partner try to play catch while moving about the room.*
3. *Now stand still with your partner across from you. Try bouncing the ball to your partner.*
4. *Try bouncing the ball to your partner while moving about the room.*
5. *You and your partner sit down facing one another.* (Each person will now have a ball.) *You and your partner each roll your balls to each other at the same time. Try to keep the two balls going without hitting each other.* Let the children experiment with that problem and then talk about solutions. Some partners will want to try to toss two balls at once and that's okay, too!

Popcorn Machine (Groups)

Equipment: Preschool indoor climber or enough cones or chairs to mark off a 4-foot to 6-foot square; one ball for each child.

This game works best using a preschool indoor climber (either a wooden or a plastic model) as the "Popcorn Machine." Put all of the balls inside the climber. Then, climb inside the Popcorn Machine. Warn the children not to climb on the popper, as it will be getting very hot. Talk about the fact that the Popcorn Machine has no lid, so the "popcorn" will be flying all over the room.

Tell the children that it is their job to pick up the popcorn and put it back in the popper as fast as possible. Remind the children that they will be moving very fast and that they should watch out for each other. Then, begin stirring the popcorn, and soon it is being popped all over the room.

After the children get the idea of the game, give them turns to be inside the Popcorn Machine. Depending on the size of the Popcorn Machine, put at least

two or three children inside the popper at one time. This is such an active game that a turn popping the corn for just one minute is plenty tiring for preschoolers.

Be creative in building your Popcorn Machine. If you do not have an indoor climber, set up chairs in a circle with the seats turned to the inside. Tumbling mats can be set on their sides—and then the popcorn will have to pop really high. Happy popping. This game is a super-screamer!

Another Helping Line (Groups)

Equipment: One ball for each child.

After dividing the class into two groups, have each group of children line up one behind the other. The children should stand with their feet wide apart. Give the first person in each line a ball. That child should pass the ball through his legs to the person behind him. When the last person in the line gets the ball she should run to the front of the line and start the passing all over again.

When you are ready to end the class, tell the children that the last person needs to take the ball, put it in the ball bag, and go sit by the door (or wait in an appropriate place). The children will need to pay close attention so they know when they are last. The teacher keeps starting new balls until each person has a chance to put away a ball.

LESSON 6

Strike and Catch (Equipment Activity)

Equipment: One ball per child.

Hold the ball in your hand. Strike it underneath so it goes straight up in the air. Try to catch the ball.

Aerobic Ball II (Warm-up)

Equipment: One ball per child. This activity may be done with music.

1. *Sit down with your knees up and your feet flat on the floor. Hold the ball in your lap. Using your feet to help you move, "walk" forward on your seat. Now try going backwards.* Repeat several times.

2. Using the counts of "out" and "in," have the children push the ball out away from themselves, and then bring the ball back in close to their bodies. Allow free exploration—the children can push the ball forward, sideways, up, down, etc.

3. *Hold the ball under one arm and move in the room. Now put the ball under your other arm.*

4. *Lie on your side, using the ball as a pillow. Raise your top leg as high as you can and bring it back down.* (Repeat several times on count with the teacher.) *Turn over on your other side and repeat the maneuver.*

5. *Hold the ball on top of your head and move any way you like.*

Nudge It (Individuals)

Equipment: One ball per child; one milk jug per child.

1. *Push the ball along on the floor using first one foot and then the other.* It is important to use words like *push*, nudge, or tap. At this point you do not want the children kicking the ball as hard as they can.

2. Show the children how to gently put their foot on the ball to stop it. Challenge the children to move their ball around the room, and, when you give the "stop" signal, to try to stop their ball with their foot. Repeat several times. Encourage the children to give each foot a turn to be the stopper.

3. Continue step 2 above, but after the children get the balls stopped they should pick them up and trade with the classmate they are standing closest to. You will need to work with the children on trading with the closest person and doing it quickly.

4. *Can you go backwards and still move the ball with your feet?*

5. Give each child a milk jug. Ask the children to try to knock their milk jug over with their ball. Suggest that they can use either their hands or their feet. The children will select their own distance in order to be successful. If the children comment that it is "too easy," then challenge them to move farther away from their jug.

6. Ask the children if they always have to be facing their jug in order to knock it over.

Feet Ball (Partners)

Equipment: One ball for every two people; one milk jug per child.

Have the children put their milk jugs away for now. Use just one ball for each pair.

1. One of the partners should stand still. The other one should try to maneuver the ball all about the room using just her feet. In so doing, the "movers" should wind around all of the "standers." Have the children switch jobs. Repeat so each person gets two turns to be a "mover."

2. The partners should face each other. Have them move the ball to each other using just their feet. If you show them how, some of the more skilled players will also be able to stop the ball with their feet. (That isn't really important for 3- and 4-year-olds. Let them be successful.)

3. Continue with Step 2, but ask the children if they always have to be facing one another.

4. Give each set of partners two milk jugs. Show them how to set up the jugs and then position themselves so they can move the ball to each other through the markers. The children can use their hands or their feet.

5. Talk to the children about how they can challenge themselves. They can either make the space between the jugs smaller, or the children can move farther away from the jugs.

6. Ask the children if they always have to be facing forward (toward the jugs).

Monster Gobble (Group)

Equipment: Ten to fifteen balls; one full-sized or queen-sized blanket or sheet.

You become the monster by crouching under a blanket. Encourage the children to feed the monster by *rolling* balls under the blanket. The monster may make all kinds of monstrous gobbling noises, and she will quickly roll the balls back out to the children.

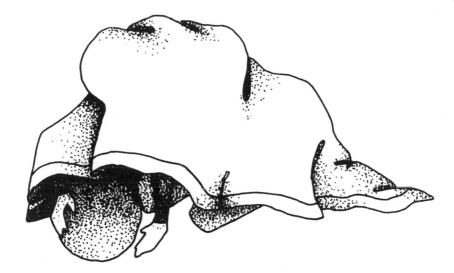

The monster may be stationary or may move about the room. Be sure to explain to the children about not jumping on the monster. Two or three children at a time may replace the teacher and become the monster. When you are ready for class to end, then you become the monster again. This time keep the balls under the blanket until you have collected them all.

Hula Hoops

INTRODUCTION

This series of lessons is designed to provide a multitude of activities centered around the use of hula hoops. While some of the activities are unique to the hula hoops, in many instances other equipment can be substituted for the hoops. For activities where the hoop is used to designate specific or individual space on the floor, you can substitute bicycle inner tubes or carpet samples. If something firmer or more "rollable" is desired, as when the hoop is held vertically on the floor, then bicycle tires can be used. When using bicycle inner tubes remember to cut out the valves before allowing the children to use them. Check the bike tires for any sharp edges. Bicycle retail shops are usually more than willing to let you carry away their discarded inner tubes and tires.

While the hula hoop is an old standard, there are now enough variations to make the purchase of hula hoops somewhat confusing. Hula hoops have traditionally been offered in physical education catalogues in three sizes: 24-inch, 30-inch, and 36-inch. (The size represents the diameter of the hoop.) If your equipment will be used exclusively by three- and four-year-olds, then the 24-inch hoops are ideal. You will want a 30-inch or 36-inch hoop for yourself, however. The 24-inch hoops actually seem a little small for the five- and six-year olds, so if your program includes that age group you would want to purchase 30-inch hoops instead of 24-inch hoops. The author has used the 30-inch hoops with three- and four-year-olds with a great deal of success. At this writing the author has discovered that at least one physical education supply catalogue is now offering a 28-inch hula hoop. Common sense suggests that the 28-inch diameter would be ideal for use with children ages three through six.

You may be tempted to sidestep the size dilemma by ordering segmented hoops. Various sizes of hoops can be made, depending on the number of short segments you put together. One definite advantage of these hoops is that any part of the hoop that is bent or broken can easily be replaced without having to discard the entire hoop. The disadvantage of segmented hoops is that with time, use, and wear, these hoops do not hold together. They tend to pop apart at the most inconvenient times.

Hula hoops can also be purchased at toy stores and department stores. These stores usually offer two size choices: 30-inches and 36-inches. (We've already been through this, right?) You will want the 30-inch hoops. The 36-inch hoops are too cumbersome for preschool youngsters. The good news is that these store-bought hoops generally have a bead or marble inside the hoop. This bead tends to balance the hoop so you get a better spin on the hoop when doing the "hula." The bad news, depending on your tolerance, is the noise.

To get an interesting feel, a different kind of spin or roll to the traditional hoop, make a very, very small hole in the hoop and inject a little water into the plastic tubing.

Before starting to use hula hoops, instruct the children about safety and care in using the hoops. They need to know that hula hoops should never be thrown. They are made of a hard plastic and they do hurt. Teach the children right away to use the hoops carefully so the hoops will keep their round shape, without a lot of bends and kinks.

If you do order hoops from an equipment supply company, save the box. The hoops can be kept in good condition by storing them and transporting them in their original box.

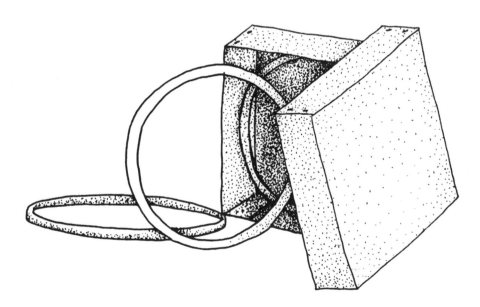

LESSON 1

Hula Hoop (Equipment Activity)

Equipment: One hula hoop per child.

As you hand out the hula hoops, ask the children if they can put the hula hoop around their waist and keep it going. After the children each have a hoop and have had a chance to experiment, demonstrate the technique for getting the hoop started.

It is a common error for novice "hula hoopers" to stand in the middle of the hoop without any part of the hoop touching them and to try to spin the hoop around themselves. It is easiest to start the hoop if you hold the hoop against the small of your back while giving it a spin.

Swaying Hoops (Warm-up)

Equipment: One hula hoop per child.

1. *Hold the hoop in two hands high over your head. Bend at the waist and sway sideways to the left and to the right.*
2. *Place the hoop on the floor. Stand on the outside of the hoop, with your side to the hoop. On two feet, jump into the hoop and out of the hoop. As the children become comfortable with this, speed up the tempo so they are jumping very rapidly.*
3. *Sit down inside the hoop. Sit cross-legged. Bend forward at the waist, and with both arms reach as far forward as possible.*

Circus Hoops (Individuals)

Equipment: One hula hoop per child.

The children can experiment with making the hula hoop twirl around various parts of their body. They might have seen someone in the circus do this.

1. *It is easiest to start the hoop on your arm: Hang the hoop on your wrist and give it a spin with your other hand. Then try to spin the hoop on your other arm.*

2. *The hoop will also spin on your neck. Bend forward at the waist and hang the hoop on your neck. Give it a quick spin with one hand.*

3. *The hoop will spin on your leg, too.* A teacher or a taller child can demonstrate this. *Balance on one leg, hold the other leg straight out, and spin the hoop on that ankle.* Preschoolers like to see this demonstrated, but usually they are too short to hold the hoop up high enough off the ground to keep it twirling.

Inside, Outside *(Individuals)*

Equipment: One hula hoop per child.

Ask the children to lay the hula hoop on the floor. Ask them to stand inside the hoop. Talk about what it means for their whole body to be inside the hoop. Then ask them to put their whole body outside the hoop. Explain to the children that while the hoop is lying on the floor, they are going to find ways to move into the hoop and out of the hoop.

1. The children will usually start by jumping into and out of the hoop. Ask them if they can jump backwards or sideways. *Can you do a spin in the air when you jump into the hoop?*

2. Challenge the children to hop on one foot. *Be sure to use the other foot sometimes. Can you hop backwards?*

3. *Can you use your hands and your feet to help you get into the hoop?* Emphasize the "feet" part, for when children hear "hands and feet" they often respond by getting down on their hands and knees. You will see mule kicks, cartwheels—the traditional one and the preschool version— frog hops, and a myriad of other wonderful responses. Remind the children that they can also be on their hands and feet with their tummies up towards the ceiling.

Ask the children to explore fancy ways of getting into and out of the hoop.

1. *What kinds of fancy things can you do with your arms or your legs while you are jumping?*
2. *Can you make a fancy shape with your arms after you land inside the hoop?*

Handshake Hoops (Partners)

Equipment: One hula hoop for every two children.

With the hoop hanging on the wrist of one of the children, the partners grasp hands as if shaking hands. The other partner should give the hoop a quick spin, and if the two gently shake hands they should be able to keep the hoop twirling. With practice the children will be able to make the hoop travel from one arm to the other. Of course, if they raise their arms too high, the hoop will fall over the "hoopster's" head. That's fun too!

Doorways (Partners)

Equipment: One hula hoop for every two children.

One of the partners should hold the hoop vertically on the floor. The challenge is for the other partner to find ways to go through the hoop "doorway."

1. *Do you always have to go forward? Can you sometimes go backwards or even sideways?*

This is an excellent activity for working on "leading body parts." Ask the children to go through the hoop and to notice which part of their body goes through the hoop first.

2. *Can you go through the hoop with your hand leading you?*

3. *Can your elbow lead you through the hoop? Make sure it stays in front all the way through.*

4. *When you go backwards through the hoop, which part of your body is leading?*

5. *See if your partner can tell you which part of your body led you through your hoop.*

   The children will tend to get very detailed with this. They will lead with their noses, thumbs, tummies, and ears. Be sure to point out all of the wonderful ideas you are seeing. This is a great awakening to body awareness.

Magic Circle (Group)

Equipment: One to six hula hoops.

The children should stand in a circle and all hold hands. The teacher should temporarily separate the hands of two players, hang the hoop on the wrist of one of the players, and have those two hold hands again.

1.

2.

Ask the children if they can find a way to get the hula hoop to travel around the circle without anyone letting go of hands. There are a couple of ways to accomplish this feat. The two players having the hoop between them need to raise their arms so the hoop drops over the head of one of them. Then that player needs to step out of the hoop—*without letting go of hands*—and move her arm so the hoop travels to the next player's arm and over his head. Another way to make the hoop travel is to first step into the hoop and then maneuver your arm so the hoop is moved up and over your head.

As the children become comfortable with moving the hoop around the circle, add more hoops to the circle. Also challenge the children to make the hoops travel in the opposite direction around the circle.

LESSON 2

Rolling Hoops (Equipment Activity)

Equipment: One hula hoop per child.

As you hand out the hula hoops, ask the children if they can stand the hoop up and roll it everywhere in the room. Caution the children to watch out for each other.

Marching Hoops (Warm-up)

Equipment: One hula hoop per child.

1. *Place the hoop on the floor. Stand outside of the hoop, facing the hoop. On two feet, jump into the hoop and out of the hoop as fast as you can.*
2. *Stand inside the hoop. Put your arms straight out and make large arm circles. Then make the arm circles going in the other direction.*
3. *Lifting your knees up high, march around the outside of the hoop. March in the other direction also.*
4. *Sit cross-legged inside the hoop. Put your arms overhead and lean as far sideways as you can. Then lean to the other side. Gently lean from side to side, feeling a gentle stretch along your side.*

Big and Small, Wide and Tall (Individuals)

Equipment: One hula hoop or carpet square per child.

1. Challenge each child to get inside his hoop and try to be as small as possible.
2. Ask the children to cover up as much floor space as possible inside the hoop. They need to spread out as much as possible, but still stay inside the hoop. Some children will be on their backs, and others will be on their tummies, so challenge them to turn over and cover the floor.
3. Ask the children to be as tall as they can inside the hoop. Point out those who are up on tiptoes—this makes them even taller!
4. Ask the children if they can be inside the hoop without covering up very much floor space. *Can you be inside the hoop and have most of your body off the floor? Don't jump up and down—hold your body still.*
5. Ask the children to make a twisted shape inside the hoop. Remind them to twist their legs, twist their arms, twist at the waist, twist their fingers, etc. *Remember, you can twist at a high level or a low level.*

6. Ask the children if they know what it means to be wide. After talking about the word *wide*, ask the children to show you what it means—but stay inside the hoop.

7. Ask the children if they know what it means to be *narrow*. After talking about the word *narrow*, challenge the children to make a narrow shape inside the hoop. *Remember, you can be narrow at a high or a low level.*

8. Ask the children to stay inside their hoop and make their body into the shape of the hoop. Ask the children if they can make another round shape.

Train Your Hoop (Individuals)

Equipment: One hula hoop per child.

Tell the children a story of how they might train their hula hoop to do tricks, just like you can train a dog to do tricks. Act as if you are rolling the hoop forward, but as you release the hoop, give it a quick spin backwards. The hoop should hit the floor 3 feet to 4 feet in front of you, and then it will roll backwards to you. When the hoop first hits the floor give a quick whistle, clap, command to make it appear as if the hoop is coming back to you on command. Then challenge the children to train their hoops. Let the children experiment for a few minutes before showing them the trick to training their hoops.

Hook the Hoop (Partners)

Equipment: One hula hoop for every two children.

Partners should stand 4 feet to 6 feet apart, facing one another. One of the partners has a hula hoop.

1. *Can you gently roll the hoop to your partner so she can catch it? Then your partner will roll the hula hoop back to you.*

2. *Now try to roll the hoop with your other hand. And your partner can try to catch the hoop with her other hand too!*

3. *Can you catch the hoop with some other part of your body besides your hands?* Point out all of the terrific ideas you see. The children can try to catch the hoop with their legs, or necks, or elbows, or fingers, or knees, or whatever!

Doubles (Partners)

Equipment: One hula hoop per child.

Partners should stand 4 feet to 8 feet apart, facing one another. Each child has a hoop. The partners should roll their hoops to each other at the same time.

Then give both hoops to one of the partners. He should try to roll both hoops at once to his partner. He can do this by having a hoop in each hand, or he can hold both hoops together in one hand. Challenge the partner to roll one hoop and then to quickly roll the other hoop after it, as if it were chasing the first hoop. This is a real challenge for the partner to catch.

Train Station (Group)

Equipment: One hula hoop per child.

Each child should stand inside his own hoop and hold it waist high. The children should then line up one behind the other. The train is connected by the children holding onto the front end of their own hoop and the back end of the hoop that is in front of them.

After the children become comfortable with moving forward, they can practice moving backwards or sideways.

The conductor can call for frequent stops and ask the "engine" (front person) to become the "caboose" (last person), so each child gets to be the leader. If one long train is too difficult, start with a few shorter trains.

LESSON 3

Train Your Hoop (Equipment Activity)

Equipment: One hula hoop per child.

Ask the children if their hoop is trained to come back to them. The children can practice spinning the hoop back to them as they learned in Lesson 2.

"Chicken Fat" (Warm-up, Partners)

Equipment: Record or tape of the music "Chicken Fat;" (*Chicken Fat* by Meredith Wilson, Kimbo Educational, or *Simplified Rhythm Stick Activities* by Laura Johnson, Kimbo Educational, 1976), record or tape player; One hula hoop for every two children.

The hoop is placed on the floor and the partners stand outside the hoop across from each other.

1. *Walk around the outside of the hoop* (**16 counts**). (Demonstrate.)
2. *Reverse directions and walk* (**16 counts**).
3. *Stand in place and march.*
4. *Forward stride jump: Stand with your feet in a forward stride. With every jump, change the foot that is forward.*
5. *Stand across from each other on the outside of the hoop. Now pick up the hoop and swing it from side to side.*
6. *Run around the outside of the hoop.*
7. *Raise the hoop over your heads and lower it over both of you.*
8. *Stand next to your partner. Hold hands and jump into and out of the hoop.*

Getting Dressed (Individuals)

Equipment: One hula hoop per child.

Tell the children that this activity is like putting a T-shirt or sweatshirt on over their head. They should hold the hoop over their head, put their arms through the hoop, put their head through the hoop, and then let the hoop drop to the floor. Step out of the hoop and repeat the action.

Start slowly and talk the children through this. Then try to get them to repeat this activity as quickly as possible. A common error for this activity is that the children will forget to step out of the hoop; they will just stay inside the hoop and raise it up and down.

Another way to "get dressed" is to stand inside the hoop and then pull it up and over your head. Then lay the hoop on the floor in front of you and jump into the hoop. Isn't this like putting on your jeans?

Up and Over (Individuals)

Equipment: One hula hoop per child.

Lay the hoop on the floor and stand outside of the hoop.

1. *Can you go over the hoop and land on the other side?*
2. *Can you go over the hoop without touching the floor in the middle of the hoop?*
3. *Can you go over the hoop and touch the floor in the middle of the hoop on your way over?* This will allow for cartwheels, mule kicks, frog jumps, etc.
4. *Can you do something fancy with your arms when you get to the other side of the hoop?*
5. Have the children move about the room, going over each hoop. Challenge them to go over each hoop in a different way. Remind the children that when you give the "stop" signal, they should stand inside the closest hoop.

Inside, Outside Together (Partners)

Equipment: One hula hoop for every two children.

The hoop should be lying on the floor.

1. *Hold hands with your partner and jump into and out of the hoop.*
2. *Can you and your partner stay connected and find another way to get into and out of the hoop?*

3. *Can you find another way to be connected to your partner and still move into and out of the hoop?*

4. *Do you always have to stay up high, or can you sometimes be down low to move into and out of the hoop?*

5. *Can you and your partner make a fancy shape together inside the hoop?*

Sharing Musical Hoops (Group)

Equipment: Music source; one hula hoop per child.

Use any music you like. Each child has a hoop, which is on the floor. The children should start standing inside their own hoop. The children should move about the room while the music is playing. When the music stops, the children should run to the nearest hoop and stand inside it. Practice doing this quickly: there are always a few who want to run to "their own" hoop.

This is a great game for practicing various locomotor movements. Assign the children to move in specific ways, for example, skipping, galloping, hopping, jumping, and galloping sideways. To further challenge the children and make it a memory game, tell the children ahead of time which body part to put inside the hoop when the music stops. For example, *"This time you are going to move by galloping. When the music stops, put just one hand inside the hula hoop."* Some children will develop a physical memory aid. For example, if they are to put their nose inside the hoop when the music stops, they will put their hand on their nose the whole time they are moving.

After the children become familiar with the moving and the memory, tell them that this time when the music is playing you will remove some hula hoops. But no one will be left out of the game! Now the children will have to *share* their hoops. As the game progresses the teacher keeps removing hoops from the game, so at every stop there are more and more children sharing one hoop. Keep varying the methods of movement and the body parts to put inside the hoops. It is fun to end the class by going for a "world record"—see how many children can share one hoop. It's easy to get twenty children to share a hoop if each person puts only their pinky finger inside the hoop!

LESSON 4

Getting Dressed (Equipment Activity)

Equipment: One hula hoop per child.

Let the children practice the "Getting Dressed" activity learned in Lesson 3.

Dancing Hoops (Warm-up)

Equipment: Music source; one hula hoop per child.

Use any fun, lively music. You can make up your own movements or use the example below. Alternate between arm movements and leg movements. Remember, you can change directions: forwards, backwards, or sideways. The easiest progression is to do arm movements while standing still. After you've shown the children some basic ideas, let them make up their own dances.

1. *Hold the hoop and gallop about the room.*
2. *Hold the hoop in front of you. Push it out and pull it in on the beat.*
3. *Lay the hoop on the floor. Stand inside it and do a forward stride jump.*
4. *Stand with the hoop held over your head. Pull the hoop down over your head and hold it shoulder high. Move the hoop up and down on the beat.*
5. *Hold the hoop in front of you. Kick one leg up so your foot goes through the middle of the hoop. Do five kicks with one foot and five kicks with the other foot.*

6. *Hold the hoop with two hands in front of you. Stand with feet shoulder-width apart. Twist your body to the left and to the right.*

Driving Lesson (Individuals)

Equipment: One hula hoop per child; record or tape player; record or tape with the music "Seven Jumps." ("Seven Jumps" is a traditional folk dance and can be found on the record *All Purpose Folk Dances* by Michael Herman, RCA Victor LPM-1623.)

Tell the children that they are going to have a driving lesson. The hula hoop will be their steering wheel. Let the children tell you what they will be driving: some will have trucks, some will have cars, and others will have motorcycles. Tell the children that they must move by galloping. Let them practice this skill briefly.

Ask the children what they should do when they are in their car or truck and they want to say "hi" to someone or they want to warn someone of danger. That's right, they honk their horn. Tell the children to listen for the horn honking on the music you will be playing. When the horn is honking they need to stop immediately and press on their own imaginary horn. Remind them that the record will make the sound, and they should not use their voices to make the honking sound.

When the music is finished, ask the drivers to park their vehicles and turn off the engine. It is fun to have a "driver's license" ready to give to each young driver.

Going Visiting (Partners)

Equipment: One hula hoop for every two children.

Half the group should hold the hoops at various angles on and slightly above the floor. The other half of the group moves about the room, going through each hoop. The challenge is to try to get the children to move differently through each hoop. The children will need several tries at this before they become conscious of leading with different body parts, etc. The teacher may need to make some specific challenges, for example, "*Can you go through the doorway with your elbow leading, and then your seat, and then your nose?*"

Revolving Door (Partners)

Equipment: One hula hoop for every two children.

One of the partners stands the hoop on the floor and *slowly* twirls it. Ask the children if they have ever seen a door that moves like this. Some will have seen a revolving door before. The other partner should try to walk through the door while it is revolving. (Talk about the word *revolving*). Then let Partner 2 have a turn to go through the door.

1. *For your next turn, see if your partner can revolve the door in the opposite direction.*

2. *Can you go through the revolving door backwards? How about sideways?*

3. Have the children travel about the room going through each revolving door.

"Pop Goes the Weasel" (Group)

Equipment: Record or tape with the music "Pop Goes The Weasel;" (*All Purpose Folk Dances* by Michael Herman. RCA Victor-LPM-1623) record or tape player; one hula hoop.

The children are in circle formation. One child is on the outside of the circle holding the hula hoop. While holding the hoop, the child moves around the outside of the circle as the music plays. On "Pop," this child drops the hoop over the head of a child standing on the circle. The child who has the hoop put over her head is the new person to go around the outside of the circle. Continue the game until each person gets a turn to go around the circle.

It is easier for the children to know who has had a turn if you start with a hula hoop for each child. Have the hoops in a stack on the outside of the circle. When Albert drops a hoop over Betty's head, Betty should leave that hoop and pick up a new hoop from the stack and continue around the circle. Albert will stand inside the hoop he dropped over Betty's head. If Betty drops the hoop over Carl's head, then Carl picks up a new hoop and Betty stands inside the hoop she dropped over Carl's head. Anyone who is standing inside a hoop has already had a turn.

LESSON 5

Balancing Act (Equipment Activity)

Equipment: One hula hoop per child.

Have the children lay the hula hoop on the floor, then stand on the hoop and try to walk around it without falling off.

1. *Can you use your arms to help you balance?*
2. *Can you go backwards around the hoop?*
3. *What about going sideways?*
4. *Can you go sideways crossing one foot over the other?*

"Pop Goes The Hula Hoop" (Warm-up)

Equipment: Record or tape with the music "Pop Goes The Weasel;" record or tape player; one hula hoop per child.

As the music is playing the children should hold the hoops above their heads while moving about the room. Whenever they hear "pop goes the weasel," they should drop the hoops over their heads and let them fall to the floor. They should immediately pick up the hoops and start moving again.

Falling Doorways (Individuals)

Equipment: One hula hoop per child.

1. *Stand the hula hoop on its edge. Try to crawl through the hoop and catch it before it falls to the floor.*
2. *Try going backwards or sideways sometimes.*
3. *Can you go through the hoop while holding on to it?*
4. Challenge the children to roll the hoop down the floor and try to crawl through the hoop while it is rolling. You may need to use tumbling mats for the more adventuresome, who will try to dive through the hoops. Caution these children to catch themselves with their hands.

Mexican Hoop Dance (Partners)

Equipment: One hula hoop for every two children; record player or tape player; record or tape with the music "La Raspa." ("La Raspa" is a traditional folk dance and can be found on the record *All Purpose Folk Dances* by Michael Herman, RCA Victor LPM-1623.)

Two children share a hoop. They are each standing on the outside of the hoop, holding the hoop with both hands and facing each other.

1. *Slide in a clockwise circle.*
2. Forward stride jump: *Stand with your feet in a forward stride. With every jump, change the foot that is in front.*
3. *Slide in a counterclockwise circle.*
4. Dip: *Bend knees and stand up straight.*

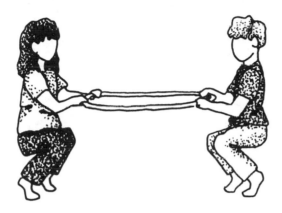

Red and Blue Relay (Group)

Equipment: Red and blue hula hoops. (if your hoops are a different color you'll need to change the name of the game); one flying disk, beanbag, or small ball for every two children.

The hoops are laid out in the following formation:

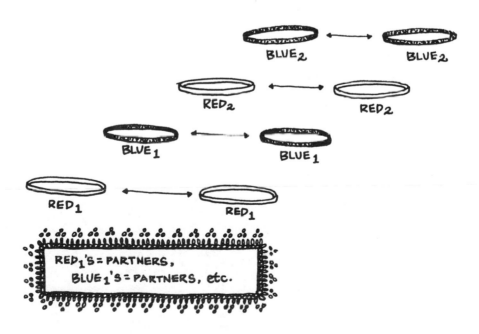

Partners stand across from each other inside their hoops, so partners will have the same color hoops. One row of hoops on one side of the room will start with each person having a flying disk.

1. The teacher calls a color, either "red" or "blue." If the teacher calls "blue," those children standing in a blue hoop and holding a flying disk should run across the room and give the disk to their partner.

2. Remind the children that they only run if they are holding the flying disk.

3. Mix up the calls when the children become familiar with the game. Call both colors at once or call the same color twice consecutively.

LESSON 6

Hats and Hoops (Equipment Activity)

Equipment: One hula hoop per child; one flying disk per child.

Point out that a flying disk can be worn as a hat. As you hand out the equipment challenge the children to stand inside their hoop and balance their hat on their head.

1. *Balance the hat on your elbow.*
2. *Balance the hat on your back.*
3. *Balance the hat on your chest.*
4. *Balance the hat on your thigh.*
5. *Balance the hat on your foot.*

Fast Flyers (Warm-up)

Equipment: One hula hoop per child; one flying disk per child.

1. *Stand inside your hoop. Hold the flying disk in one hand, and with that arm make big arm circles. Repeat with your other arm.*
2. *Stand inside your hoop. Hold the disk in two hands above your head. Jump with a wide stride: first jump with your feet together, then with your feet shoulder-width apart, then together, then apart.*
3. *Lie on your back inside the hoop, knees up and feet flat on the floor. Hold the disk in two hands on your chest. Push it up and pull it down.* Repeat several times.
4. *Stay in the same position* (as Step 3). *Hold the disk on your chest. Kick one leg straight up, then bring it back to the starting position. Kick up your other leg,* etc.
5. *Stand inside your hoop. Hold your disk as if it were a tambourine. Clap your hands over your head on the beat.*

Target Practice (Individuals)

Equipment: One hula hoop per child; one flying disk per child.

The children can either lay the hoop on the floor or prop it against the wall.

1. *Try to toss the disk into the hoop.* The children can choose their own distance from the hoop.
2. *Be sure to use the other hand sometimes.*
3. *Can you turn your back to the hoop and toss the disk through your legs?*

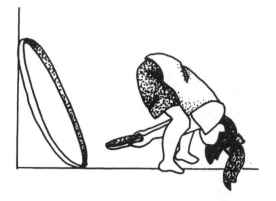

4. *Can you toss the disk backwards over your head?*

5. *Can you make up some new ways to get the disk into the hoop?*

Slam Dunk (Partners)

Equipment: One hula hoop for every two children; one 6-inch to 9-inch
ball for every two children.

One child will hold the hoop as if it were a basketball hoop. She should hold
the hoop to her side so that her partner will not be shooting baskets directly at
her face.

Her partner can take several turns shooting her "basketball" at the "basketball hoop." She can ask her partner to raise or lower the hoop, and she can
even try to "slam dunk" the ball.

Memory Game (Group)

Equipment: At least two different colors of hoops, several of each.

Lay the hoops in a row on the floor, alternating the two colors. Line the
children up at one end of the row of hoops. The children should move individually

through the row of hoops, stepping into each hoop in turn and performing a specific task according to the color of the hoop. For example:

1. *When you are inside a blue hoop jump on two feet. When you are inside a red hoop hop on one foot.*
2. *When you are inside a blue hoop hold both arms straight up in the air. When you are inside a red hoop put your hands on your hips.*
3. *When you are inside a blue hoop jump on two feet. When you are inside a red hoop put your hands on your hips.*

Arranging the hoops in a random pattern will increase the difficulty of the task. Adding another color will increase the difficulty of the task.

To eliminate a lot of standing and waiting try to have several rows of hoops. Six hoops in a row will be sufficient.

Cave Exploring (Group)

Equipment: Four to six hula hoops; tumbling mat or carpeted floor.

The teacher and an assistant or two should hold four to six hula hoops vertically on a tumbling mat. There should be about one foot between each hoop.

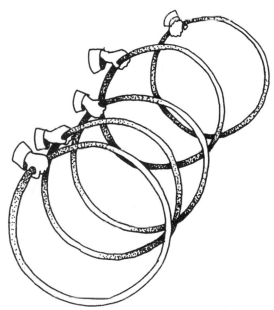

1. Challenge the children to move through this "cave" without touching the sides of the cave.
2. Have the children try to move through the cave backwards.
3. While still holding the hoops vertically, gently roll the hoops back and forth, so it appears as if the tunnel is moving. Challenge the children to explore this moving tunnel.
4. There could be obstacles at the end of the tunnel, such as a balance beam.

Scoops and Tennis Balls

INTRODUCTION

This series of lessons is designed for the use of plastic scoops cut from gallon-size bleach or fabric softener jugs. The scoops can likewise be made from gallon milk jugs, but they will not be as sturdy and are less desirable. Remove the lids and use those in some other recycling project.

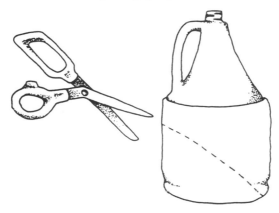

It will not take long to secure a sufficient number of scoops if you ask your organization's families to donate the containers. Daycare centers should be a tremendous source of bleach bottles. Or ask your local recycling center to save a few dozen of the containers for you.

Sometimes it is useful to color-code the scoops. There are a couple of ways to do this. You can paint the scoops using spray paint or tempera paint. The scoops can be painted a solid color, or you can use a screen to paint stars, circles, or other fun shapes. Or, you can put colored stripes on the scoop using inch-wide gymnasium tape. Put two or three stripes on each scoop. Whichever method you use, put only one color or one shape on each scoop.

The great thing about tennis balls is that they fit the hands of preschoolers. There are hundreds of used tennis balls out there. In fact, you do not want new tennis balls, since they will be too lively. The used balls will not have as much bounce and will therefore be easier to control. Ask your local racquet club or athletic club to post a sign asking members to donate used tennis balls. Perhaps local sporting goods stores would post a similar sign, right next to the cans of new tennis balls they hope to sell.

The children will be developing hand-eye coordination, and using a manipulative always makes the activity more challenging. Be sure to encourage the children to use the manipulative with both their right and left hands.

As before, each lesson will have five parts:

1. Equipment Activity—a simple challenge for the children while you are handing out the equipment.

2. Warm-up—to get the whole body loosened up and ready to move.

3. Individual Challenges—so the children can explore alone together.

4. Partner Challenges—for more complex challenges and to learn to work cooperatively.

5. Group Activities—for silly fun to end the lesson.

Allow ample time for the children to explore each challenge. Review starting and stopping signals before handing out the equipment.

LESSON 1

Swirling Balls (Equipment Activity)

Equipment: One scoop and one tennis ball per child.

The teacher can first give one scoop to each child. The children should hold the scoop in front of them, ready to receive a tennis ball. As the children receive their tennis ball, they should gently swirl the ball inside the scoop.

1. *Now try to make the ball swirl in the other direction.*
2. *Can you hold the scoop in your other hand and swirl the ball?*
3. *Now can you make the ball swirl in the other direction?*

Squeezees (Warm-up)

Equipment: One tennis ball per child. Have the children simply place the scoop on the floor behind them.

1. *Hold the ball in one hand high above your head. Squeeze the ball as hard as you can. Keep the ball high above your head!*
2. *Now try squeezing the ball with your other hand! Keep it high above your head!*
3. *Put the ball between your knees. Squeeze the ball as hard as you can with your knees.*
4. *Hold the ball between your two hands in front of your chest. Push your two hands together and squeeze the ball as hard as you can.*
5. *Sit down with your feet flat on the floor and your knees up. Put the ball between the arches of your feet. Push your feet together and try to squeeze the ball.*

6. *While still sitting down, place the ball on the floor beside one hip. With your hand, push down on the ball as hard as you can. Put the ball beside your other hip and push down with your other hand.*

Tossing Hand, Catching Hand (Individuals)

Equipment: One scoop and one tennis ball per child.

Talk to the children about holding the scoop in one hand and using it like a baseball glove. Explain that each hand will have a special job to do. The hand they are holding the scoop with is their "catching hand;" the hand they toss the ball with is their "tossing hand."

1. *Toss the ball with your hand and catch it with your scoop.* You may want to challenge some to toss the ball higher, and others to toss the ball lower so they can catch it.
2. *Put the scoop in the other hand. Now toss and catch.*
3. *Try to make the ball bounce one time on the floor before you catch it.*
4. *Now try to bounce the ball with your other hand and catch with your other hand.*

Explain to the children that now only one hand at a time gets to do the work. *Put the ball inside the scoop. Hold the scoop with one hand.*

1. *Start with the ball inside the scoop and toss the ball up in the air and catch it with the scoop.*

2. *Try tossing and catching with the other hand.*

The children should put the ball inside their scoop. They will carry the ball in their scoop as they move in various ways about the room.

1. *See if you can carry the ball while galloping. Remember to watch out for each other!*
2. *Try moving backwards while holding the scoop in the other hand.*
3. *Hold the scoop high and tiptoe about the room.*
4. *Find a way to move while holding the scoop very low.*

Tossing Hand, Catching Hand With My Friend (Partners)

Equipment: Each child needs one scoop. Partners may share a tennis ball.

When the children stop moving (as in the last step of the previous activity) have them sit down with the person they are closest to. That person will be their partner. Collect one of the tennis balls from each pair. Explain that once again the children are going to give each hand a special job to do: one hand will be the "catching hand" and the other hand will be the "tossing hand."

1. The children should sit down facing one another. *Using the tossing hand, roll the ball on the floor to your partner. Try to get the ball to roll into your partner's scoop.* The partner should use his "catching hand" to scoop up the ball. The children may have the tendency to scoop the ball up with one hand, lay down the scoop, and use that same hand to roll the ball. Encourage the children to give each hand a job to do.

2. *Put the scoop in the other hand and now roll the ball with the other hand.*

3. *Try standing up and rolling the ball to each other.*

4. *Can you do any special tricks? Can you stand with your back to your partner and roll the ball to your partner through your legs?*

5. Show the children how to make a soft underhand toss. Have the children try to gently toss the ball to each other with their tossing hand and catch the ball with their catching hand.

6. Repeat Step 5 above with the scoop in the other hand.

Pass the Peas (Group)

Equipment: Ten to twenty tennis balls; one scoop per child, two to four containers for the tennis balls.

The children line up side by side. Each child has a scoop. Place a collecting container by the last person in the line. The teacher will stand by the first person

in line. Drop a tennis ball into the first person's scoop. That person should dump the ball into the scoop of the second person, and so on down the line. When the last person receives the tennis ball he should dump it into the collecting container. Keep playing until all of the balls have been collected.

To make the game last longer the teacher may grab the bucket at the end of the line and start the tennis balls all over again. Also, once the children have played this game once, let the first person start with a bucket of balls and start them on his own.

The children can also be divided into smaller groups for passing the balls. Then the game can be repeated until every person has had a chance to be the starter. When the last person has all of the balls he can run with the bucket to the front of the line and start passing the balls all over again.

LESSON 2

Helmet Swirl (Equipment Activity)

Equipment: One scoop and one tennis ball per child.

First give each child a scoop. As you do so, instruct the children to put the scoop on their head, as if it were a helmet. It will really inspire the children if you are wearing a helmet!

Then, go back through the group giving each child a tennis ball. Remind the children of how they can swirl the ball inside the scoop. But this time they are to put the ball inside the scoop, put the scoop back on their head, and try to swirl the ball inside their helmet.

Pumping Up (Warm-up)

Equipment: One tennis ball per child. Have the children simply place the scoop on the floor behind them.

1. *Hold the ball in one hand. Repeatedly, with rhythm, push that hand up and down. Repeat this with the other hand.*
2. *Make the ball travel around your waist. Hold it in one hand, put that hand behind your back and then put the ball in the other hand. Then switch hands again in front of the body.* When you are demonstrating this to the students be sure to turn around so they can actually see you put the ball in your other hand behind your back.
3. *Try to make the ball travel around your waist going in the other direction.*
4. *Put your feet together. Make the ball travel around your feet just as you made it go around your waist. Then try going in the other direction.*

5. *Hold the ball in your left hand. Hold that arm up high and straight. Keep your feet on the floor and gently lean to the right, bending as far sideways as you can.* Repeat several times. *Now try it with the ball in your other hand.*

6. *Hold the ball straight out in front of you. Using either foot, try to kick the ball. Do not let go of the ball. Keep raising the ball higher so you have to kick higher. Be sure to give the other foot a turn to kick.*

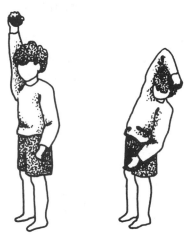

Ice Cream Cones! *(Individuals)*

Equipment: One scoop and one tennis ball per child.

1. *Start with the ball inside the scoop. Toss the ball up and catch it with the scoop. After several tries be sure to give the other hand a chance to play.*

2. *Turn the scoop over so the small opening of the jug is on top. Place the tennis ball on top of the small jug opening. This creates an ice cream cone!* Challenge the children to walk about without losing their ice cream.

3. *Hold the ice cream cone in the other hand and walk.*

4. *Hold the ice cream cone with your first hand. Now try walking backwards. Watch out for each other.*

5. *Can you find another way to move without losing your ice cream?*

Double Dips (Partners)

Equipment: One scoop and one tennis ball per child.

1. The partners should face each other, each with their own ice cream cone. Challenge the partners to trade ice cream cones without losing their ice cream. Note: The children are not just trading tennis balls, but should trade both the scoop and ball together.

2. *Partners will need to help each other set this up. We are now going to wear the ice cream on our heads! Again, wear the scoop as a helmet. Your partner should help you put the ice cream on top of the cone.* The adventurous will try to walk with their ice cream cone heads.

3. *Sit down facing your partner. Both of you at once try to roll the ball into your partner's scoop. Remember, you are going to roll the ball with one hand and scoop the ball up with the other hand.* After the children have tried this a bit, ask them what they have to do so the balls don't hit each other.

4. *Switch hands so the other hand gets to be the roller.* If the children comment that the activity is "too easy," challenge them to move farther apart.

5. The partners should stand facing each other, each with a scoop and a ball. They should each toss their ball to each other at the same time. After some practice, talk to the children about how to do this without the balls colliding. One ball can be tossed higher than the other or the balls can be tossed beside each other.

6. *Try this using your other hand as the tossing hand.*

Ice Cream Race (Partners)

Equipment: One scoop for each child; one tennis ball for each set of partners; line markers or tape for marking the floor.

Partners should stand across the room from each other. The starting partners on one side of the room should have the "ice cream" balanced on their "cone." The waiting partners on the other side of the room should stand with the big open end of the scoop ready to receive the ball.

On a signal, the starting partner moves across the room as quickly as possible and dumps the ice cream into the partner's scoop. The skills, attitudes, and personalities of the children will determine whether you have the children start over if they drop their ice cream on the way.

Then the players change starting places so the other partner gets to be the starting partner this time.

Ice Cream Flavors (Group)

Equipment: One color-coded scoop per child, or various colored spots for the children to stand on; one tennis ball per child.

All of the children should line up side-by-side holding their "ice cream cones." The color of the scoop or the color of the spot on which the child is standing will determine the flavor of ice cream the child has. When her flavor is called she should move across the room as quickly as possible and wait at the stopping line.

Carrying the ice cream on the cone may become too frustrating for the children. At that point, simply have the children carry the ice cream inside the scoop.

The game can be much less structured if no color codes are used. The children can simply imagine what flavor of ice cream they have; when that flavor is called they should move across the room.

LESSON 3

Free Exploration (Equipment Activity)

Equipment: One scoop and one tennis ball per child.

Allow free exploration. Let the children try their favorite activity with the scoop and ball or, better yet, make up a new activity.

Tennis Ball Tune-up (Warm-up)

Equipment: One tennis ball per person. Have the children place the scoop on the floor behind them.

1. *Stand with your feet shoulder-width apart. Hold the tennis ball with two hands high over your head. Gently lean backwards from the waist and then stand up straight again. Repeat this several times.*

2. *Keep standing with your feet shoulder-width apart and lean forward and down. Put the ball behind you by placing the ball on the floor through your legs. Turn around, pick up the ball, and repeat.*

3. *Hold the ball in one hand and draw circles in the air. Switch hands. Then put the ball back into your first hand and draw circles in the other direction. Again, give the other hand a turn.*

4. *Hold the tennis ball with both hands straight out in front of you. Quickly pull the ball in close to your tummy; then push the ball out hard. Do several quick repetitions.*

5. *Hold the ball between your feet. See if you can jump up and down without losing the ball.*

Super Scoops (Individuals)

Equipment: One scoop and one tennis ball per child.

1. *Place the tennis ball on the floor. With a quick scooping motion, try to scoop the ball up and into the scoop. Be sure to give each hand a turn to do the scooping.*
2. *Place the ball on the floor. Quickly scoop it up, and then toss the ball into the air and catch it. Give your other hand a turn.*
3. *Stand with your feet in a wide stride. Put the ball on the floor between your feet. Turn your scoop around so you are scooping backwards, and try to scoop up the tennis ball between your feet.*

4. *Place the tennis ball on the floor. Place the wide, open end of the scoop over the ball* (the jug will be in a standing-up position) *and "pull" the ball all around the room.* Caution the children to watch out for each other.
5. *Bounce the ball high, and when it comes down catch it with the scoop. Switch hands.*
6. *Hold the ball on the scoop as if it were an ice cream cone. With a quick wrist motion flip the scoop over. The ball should fall off the "cone" and into the "scoop."*
7. *Place the ball into your scoop. Tip the scoop so the ball falls out and bounces. As the ball bounces up, catch it with the scoop.*

Buddy Scoops (Partners)

Equipment: One scoop each child; one tennis ball for each set of partners.

1. *Partners should stand facing one another. Try to bounce the ball to your partner.*
2. *Use the scoop to toss the ball to your partner. Sometimes let your other hand hold the scoop.* It will be easier for the children to catch the ball if their partner tosses it a little bit high.
3. *Put the ball on the floor. Try to gently push it with your foot to your partner's scoop. Sometimes use your other foot to push the ball.*
4. *Try to find other ways to get the ball to your partner.*

5. *You and your partner stand close together. One person starts with the ball in his scoop. He should tip the scoop so the ball falls out and bounces. As the ball bounces up, his partner should catch it with his scoop.*

6. *Partners should stand close together. They should very rapidly dump the tennis ball back and forth into each other's scoop.*

Hot Potato Scoops (Group)

Equipment: One scoop per child; ten to twenty tennis balls.

The children should sit in a circle, each child holding a scoop. You sit in the circle also, with all of the tennis balls behind you.

Dump the ball into the scoop of the person at your right, with the instructions to keep the ball going around the circle as fast as possible. Add one ball at a time. Occasionally instruct the group to change the direction of the passing.

If you use this game at the end of class, then just eliminate one ball at a time until you have collected all of the balls.

Fill It Up (Group)

Equipment: One scoop per child; as many tennis balls as possible; one or two large containers for the tennis balls.

The children may be standing side by side in one or two lines, but they will all be working together. Scatter all of the tennis balls at random throughout the room. Place one empty bucket in the center of the room.

On the signal, the children should move about the room scooping up the tennis balls as quickly as possible and running to dump them into the bucket. The children should use only their scoops to pick up the balls. You may set the limit of allowing the children to pick up only one ball at a time and run it to the bucket before they go back and scoop up another ball.

The children will enjoy repeating the activity several times, each time trying to do it faster.

SECTION V

Bean-bags

INTRODUCTION

The following lessons are designed for the use of beanbags. Beanbags are great for preschoolers—they generally travel slower than balls and thus are easier for preschoolers to see and catch. The pliability or "give" of the beanbags makes them easier for preschoolers to catch and to throw. The softness of the beanbags makes them very safe, and any sense of fear is virtually eliminated.

A beanbag is also extremely versatile: it can be used to help preschoolers learn about hand-eye coordination, foot-eye coordination, balancing, body part awareness, and moving at different levels. Beanbags can be used, or substituted for other equipment, in a wide variety of games. Keep a box of beanbags handy—you'll be amazed at how often you find a use for them.

Beanbags are very easy to make. For general use, the author recommends beanbags that are 4 inches to 5 inches in width. Beanbags have traditionally been made in a square shape, but the children could have additional learning experiences if the beanbags are made in triangular and circular shapes. (Remember to cut the fabric one inch larger than the desired finished size. This allows for a half-inch seam.) The author has also used mini-bags, which are 1½ inches to 2 inches wide. The mini-bags mimic the more expensive "foot bags" sold in toy or sporting goods stores. Using these mini-bags changes the dynamics of the movement responses you will see from the children.

Denim and corduroy are excellent fabrics for beanbags. Have fun making the bags. For example, you might keep the outside pocket intact when cutting pieces from old blue jeans, so when the beanbag is finished it has an outside pocket. For the trendy set, it's fun to keep an original label intact.

Beanbags can be filled with a variety of materials, including corn, rice, pinto beans, soy beans, or lentils. The beanbags are softer if they are filled with a finer substance, such as rice or lentils, rather than the coarser corn or pinto beans. Be sure to keep the beanbags dry.

If you do not sew, there are still a number of possibilities for having the beanbags made. In addition to asking your local parent volunteers, check with your local middle school or high school home economics class. This would be a terrific project for a beginning sewing class. Seamstresses at your local senior citizen center are another possibility.

As much as possible, it is important to start the class by giving each child his own piece of equipment. Preschoolers understandably have a "hands-on" mentality. If they can start immediately with their own equipment, they will then be ready to join a group activity at the end of the class.

LESSON 1

Hand Shuffle (Equipment Activity)

Equipment: One beanbag per child.

As rapidly as possible, dump the beanbag from one hand to the other in a quick, repetitive motion.

Jumpin' and Turnin' (Warm-up)

Equipment: One beanbag per child. This activity may be done with music. Music source is optional.

1. *Hold the beanbag in one hand. Pump that arm up and down as if you are lifting weights. Now do it with your other arm.*
2. *Hold the beanbag straight out in front of you. Kick one leg straight up, trying to kick the beanbag—but do not let go of the beanbag. You guessed it! Now try the other leg.*
3. *Hold the beanbag in one hand, and make large arm circles with that arm. Now do it with your other arm.*
4. *Hold the beanbag next to your tummy while jumping up and down as high as you can in your own space.*
5. *Hold the beanbag and make large arm circles, but this time make the circles going backwards.*
6. *Hold the beanbag on top of your head and run in place.*

Tossin' and Turnin' (Individuals)

Equipment: One beanbag per child.

1. *Try to stay in your own space and toss the beanbag up in the air and catch it.* Some children will need to be challenged to toss the beanbag higher, while others will need to be encouraged to not toss quite so high in order to successfully catch the beanbag.
2. *Toss the beanbag into the air and try turning yourself half way around before catching the bag.* Advise the children to only do this three times and then sit down. After more than three tries they'll probably become dizzy.
3. *Toss the beanbag and clap your hands as many times as you can before catching the bag.*
4. *Toss the beanbag, then tap your head and tummy before catching the beanbag.* Challenge the group to make up their own tapping sequence before catching the beanbag. The possibilities are endless. For example: Toss the bag, tap your tummy, then your knees, then catch the bag. Some

students may actually be able to tap a sequence of three body parts before catching the beanbag.

Beanbag Balance (Individuals)

Equipment: One beanbag per child.

Talk with the children about what it means to balance a beanbag on their head. *To balance something means to make it stay in place without holding it there.* Have the children practice holding the beanbag on their head. Then have them take their hands away and explain that they are now balancing the beanbag.

1. *What happens if you look down at the floor? What happens if you look up at the ceiling? That's right, the beanbag falls off your head. Where do you need to look and how do you have to hold your head if you want to balance the beanbag there? That's right, you need to look straight ahead and hold your head straight and still.*

2. *Where else on your body can you balance the beanbag?* As you point out all of the neat things you are seeing, the children will try them. You should see the beanbags balancing on backs of hands, knees, shoulders, elbows, feet, tummies, backs, hips, calves, seats, etc.

3. The next step is to challenge the children to move about the room while balancing the beanbags on various body parts. *Do you always have to be standing? Is it easier to balance the bag on your tummy if you lie down on your back? Then how will you move?*

4. *What's the easiest way to balance the beanbag on your knee? Maybe by sitting down with your legs out in front of you. Then how will you move?*

A Slide and a Glide, Give It a Ride! (Partners)

Equipment: One beanbag for every two children.

1. *Sit on the floor facing your partner. Slide the beanbag back and forth on the floor to each other.*

2. *Can you turn your back to your partner and slide the beanbag through your legs to her?*

3. *Can you use your foot to push the beanbag over to your partner? How about your other foot?*

4. *While sitting, can you gently toss the beanbag to your partner?* Show the children how to do a soft underhand toss. *Can you toss the bag with your other hand?*

5. *Now try tossing the beanbag to each other while standing up.*

Color Race (Group)

Equipment: One beanbag for each child, with an assortment of different colored beanbags; cones or gym tape for making lines.

The children should line up side by side at one end of the room. Each child should be holding his own beanbag. Discuss with the children the colors of their beanbags. Tell the children that when you call their color, they are to run as fast as possible to the line on the other side of the room.

Repeat the activity several times. Then ask the children to trade beanbags with another person so they have a different color bag.

LESSON 2

Toss and Catch by Myself (Equipment Activity)

Equipment: One beanbag per child.

Try to stay in your own space while tossing and catching the beanbag.

Tummy and Knees, If You Please (Warm-up)

Equipment: One beanbag per child.

1. (Standing.) *Hold the bag in one hand. Pass the bag behind your back and grab it with the other hand. Now pass it to your other hand in front of your tummy, and start over again.*

2. *Stop the beanbag. Now make it go around your tummy in the other direction.*
3. *Hold the beanbag next to your tummy and jump up and down. Jump first with your feet in a wide stride, then feet together, then feet wide.* Have the children jump several times.
4. *Stand with your feet together. Pass the beanbag around your knees. Pass it quickly, then stop and pass it in the other direction.*
5. *Hold the beanbag between your knees. Try to hold the beanbag with your knees while you jump up and down in place.*

Bending Backbone Beanbag Pass (Individuals)

Equipment: One beanbag per child; one carpet sample per child (or tumbling mats or a carpeted floor).

1. *Sit down with your legs together and straight out in front of you. The carpet sample should be on the floor directly behind you, so when you roll backwards your back will be cushioned by the carpet.*
2. *Hold the beanbag with your feet. Roll backwards onto your back, then up onto your shoulders. Lift your legs and reach back behind your head with your feet, keeping your legs straight. Drop the beanbag onto the floor behind your head.*
3. *Sit up. Leave the bag on the floor behind you.*
4. *Repeat the roll backwards. Try to pick up the beanbag with your feet. You will have to turn your head so you can see the beanbag.*

This will provide an opportunity to speak with the children about their backbone. Ask the children to curl up and discover how their backbone can bend. But it cannot very safely bend in the other direction: Show this by having the children stand up and try to bend backwards. Can they feel all of the little bones that together make up their backbone?

Beanbag Body Toss (Individuals)

Equipment: One beanbag per child.

1. *Toss and catch the beanbag with one hand. Then try the other hand. Give each hand several turns.*
2. *Do you remember all of the places where you can balance a beanbag? Let's do a quick review. As I call out a body part, try balancing the bag there: head, knee, back, tummy (etc.).*
3. *Now try balancing the beanbag on your head. Then gently tilt your head so the beanbag falls off your head into your hands. Balance the bag on your shoulder. Gently lean forward so the bag falls into your hands. Place the beanbag on top of your foot. Give a gentle kick so the bag comes up to*

your hands. Where else can you balance the bag and then toss it to your hands?

Beanbag Body Toss for Two (Partners)

Equipment: One beanbag for every two children.

Partners stand facing each other. One partner should start with the beanbag. She should place the beanbag on her head. Challenge her to toss the bag to her partner by jumping or giving a quick nod of the head.

The partners should take turns placing the beanbag on various body parts and then tossing the bag with that body part. Let the children share some of their discoveries with the group.

Double Bending Backbone Beanbag Pass (Partners)

Equipment: One beanbag for every two children; one carpet sample for
each child (or tumbling mats or a carpeted floor).

Partners start sitting back-to-back. Then they need to slide far enough away from each other so each of them can lie on his back. They should both now be lying on their backs, head-to-head, but without their heads touching.

One of the partners holds the beanbag between his feet. He then rolls backwards and passes the bag to his partner's feet. His partner will have also rolled backwards and will have his feet up in the air waiting to receive the beanbag.

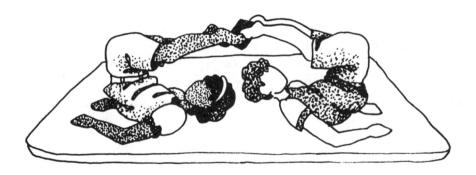

Beanbag Stack (Group)

Equipment: Twelve to twenty beanbags.

1. Divide the class into two groups. The children in each group should sit side by side, facing the other group, with a distance of 3 feet or more between the groups. Each group starts with an equal number of beanbags. The first person in each group has a stack of beanbags in front of her. Her counterpart will be sitting straight across from her.

2. On the signal "Go," the first person picks up one beanbag and passes it to the person next to her. Each person passes the bag to the person next to him or her as rapidly as possible. As soon as the leader has passed one beanbag, she immediately picks up another bag and starts passing it down the line.

3. The last person in the group has the job of stacking the beanbags on top of each other as soon as he receives them. The winning team is the first team to get all of the beanbags stacked into a single stack without the stack falling over and without anyone holding it up.

4. The last player goes to the head of the line and becomes the leader. Everyone moves down one space. Continue the game until every player has had a turn to stack the beanbags.

LESSON 3

Hurry, Scurry Beanbag Balance (Equipment Activity)

Equipment: One beanbag per child.

The children balance the beanbag on as many body parts as they can before you say "Stop."

Squeeze If You Please (Warm-up)

Equipment: One beanbag per child.

1. *Hold the beanbag in one hand. Hold it up high in the air and squeeze the bag as hard as you can. Try it with the other hand.*
2. *Lie on your back with your feet flat on the floor and your knees up. Hold the beanbag between your feet. Alternately raise your feet up and put them back down on the floor, all the while holding the beanbag between your feet.*
3. *Hold the beanbag between your upper arm and forearm. Squeeze! (I can tell by looking at your face how hard you are squeezing the beanbag!) Try it on the other side, too.*
4. *Put the beanbag behind your knee. Bend your lower leg upward and squeeze the beanbag. Repeat with your other leg.*
5. *Put the beanbag between your two palms, and push your palms together in front of your chest.*
6. *Put the beanbag on the floor. Put one foot on the bag and push down as hard as you can. Then try the other foot.*

Heels Over Head (Individuals)

Equipment: One beanbag per child.

1. *Hold the beanbag with your heels. Hold just part of the beanbag with your heels; let most of the beanbag extend behind your heels. Give a quick jump and let go of the beanbag, tossing it forward over your head.*
2. *After you learn to toss the bag over your head, the next challenge is to try to catch it!*

Under the Bridge (Individuals)

Equipment: One beanbag per child.

1. *Stand in a wide stride position. Put the beanbag on the floor in front of you. Keep your hand on the beanbag the whole time and gently push it*

backward through your legs. Do not toss the bag! The children should try to keep their legs straight, and if they do so they will feel a stretch in the back of their legs.

2. *Still in a wide stride position, jump and turn half way around. Try to land in a wide stride too.*

3. *Now, without moving your feet, bend over and pick up the beanbag. Push the beanbag through your legs again. This time when you jump, turn in the other direction.*

Target Throw (Partners)

Equipment: One or two beanbags for every two children; one milk jug for every two children.

One partner starts with the two beanbags and gets to be the "tosser." Her partner is the "helper." The helper should set the milk jug up just a few feet away from the tosser. The tosser gets two turns to toss the beanbag at the milk jug, trying to knock it over. It is the helper's job to set the jug up when it is knocked over. After the tosser has tossed both of her beanbags, she should trade jobs with the helper.

Encourage the tosser to move farther away from the target. Challenge the children to try some fancy tosses, such as backwards through the legs. Is the other hand getting a turn to toss?

Other targets can be used, such as hula hoops or carpet squares. Then the challenge is to toss the beanbag onto or through the target.

Ice Skating (Partners)

Equipment: Two beanbags for every two children.

Set the stage by having the children imagine that the floor is all ice. And if the floor is ice, then it must be cold, so everyone will have to (pretend to) put on their warmest coat, a hat, a scarf, and mittens. *What will you use for ice skates? That's right, beanbag ice skates! Put one beanbag under each foot. There is no need to tie them on, for if you just press down and slide your feet you can glide all over the ice.*

Give each partner a quick turn. On the second turn, invite the children to do some fancy ice skating. *Can you skate backwards? Can you hold one arm gracefully in the air and do a turn? Can you crouch down low and skate? Can you skate by crossing one leg in front of the other?*

Cookie Jar (Group)

Equipment: One beanbag per child; a space marker for each child would be helpful but is not necessary.

1. Lay five or six beanbags on the floor in a circle pattern. You stand inside the ring of beanbags. The children form an even bigger circle around the outside of the beanbag ring. If you have a floor marker or space marker

for each child, it is helpful to have each child stand on or beside his marker. This will help the children to maintain the large outer circle.

2. You enact the part of a parent busy in the kitchen baking cookies and setting them out to cool. But it is very hard for the children to leave the cookies alone. In fact, the children keep trying to snitch a cookie when their parent isn't looking.

3. When the children are first learning the game, you can call the names of three or four children at a time who will attempt to move in and pick up a "cookie" without being tagged by the teacher. If they are tagged by the teacher, they need to put the cookie back. If they succeed in getting back to their space with the cookie, they can keep it. Continue the game until each child has had a turn to try to snitch a cookie.

4. After the children have played once, you may try the game without calling the names of the "snitchers." Let the children just go into the "kitchen" at random. This will also give them the opportunity to be more successful in their search for cookies!

5. The more adventurous children will want to have a turn to be the baker. To speed up the game, have at least two bakers in the kitchen at the same time. If your group has more than twelve children, you may want to set up two separate games of Cookie Jar. You can then stand on the outside and control both games by calling the names of the cookie snitchers.

LESSON 4

Toss Across (Equipment Activity)

Equipment: One beanbag per child.

Hold the beanbag in one hand. Toss the beanbag up in the air and in a rainbow pathway across to your other hand. Now toss the beanbag back to your other hand, but always toss in a rainbow pathway.

Stretch and Reach (Warm-up)

Equipment: One beanbag per child.

1. *Lie on your back using the beanbag as a pillow. Roll back so your legs and hips are off the floor and "bicycle" away. Don't bump your nose with your knee!*

2. *Leave the beanbag on the floor. Get on your hands and knees, with the beanbag by your head. Do an elementary push-up (Stay up on your knees, but bend your arms to lower your upper body towards the floor.) Touch your nose to the beanbag. Do as many push-ups as you can.*

3. *Sit up with your feet flat on the floor and your knees bent. Hold the beanbag between your knees. Put your hands on the floor beside your hips. Lower your knees to the floor on your right; bring your knees back to the center position; lower your knees to the floor on your left; return to the center position, (etc.).*

1.

2.

4. *Get on your hands and knees. Place the beanbag on the small of your back. Arch your back so your tummy "sags" towards the floor. Then pull your tummy in, and round your back like a mad cat. Repeat several times.*

5. *Hold the beanbag in one hand. Hold that arm straight up in the air. Then, keeping your elbow pointing towards the ceiling, drop your hand behind your head. Keep hold of the beanbag. With your other hand reach behind your back and try to take the beanbag out of your other hand. Do this two times, and then start with the beanbag in the other hand.*

Mule Kick (Individuals)

Equipment: One beanbag per child; a carpeted surface or tumbling mats; spot marker for each child.

1. The children start on their hands and knees. They should put the beanbag on their hips. The exercise will be more difficult if the beanbag is placed on the small of the back.

2. The children should kick themselves up with their feet so their hips come above their heads. (When the children first try this you will want a safe surface, such as carpeting or tumbling mats.) The beanbag should fly off their hips and land on the floor in front of their heads.

3. With a little practice, the children are able to take this one step further. Place a spot marker, hula hoop, or carpet square on the floor in front of each person. The object then is to get the beanbag to land on the spot marker.

Wiggle and Squiggle (Individuals)

Equipment: One beanbag per child.

The children should start on their hands and knees. Don't let them sag backwards at the hips, but be sure they are up on their knees. The children should place the beanbag on their hips. While staying on their hands and knees, the children should try to wiggle and squiggle to get the beanbag to fall off their back.

Back Bend (Individuals)

Equipment: One beanbag per child.

The children should stand with their feet in a wide stride.

1. *Hold the beanbag with both hands high over your head. Keep your arms above your head and bend backwards as far as you can. Drop the beanbag onto the floor behind you.*

2. *Keeping your feet in a wide stride, stand up straight. Now, without moving your feet, bend down and reach through your legs to pick up the beanbag.*

3. *Another way to pick up the beanbag is to keep your feet wide, but bend to the right (or left), reach around—not through—your leg, and pick up the beanbag. Be sure to also try reaching around the other leg.*

Moving Catch (Partners)

Equipment: One beanbag for every two children.

Each child will need to have a partner. Have the partners try to toss the beanbag to one another while both are moving about the room. Remind the children to start by moving slowly and tossing gently.

As the children experience success, challenge them to move backwards or sideways.

Tandem Tossing (Partners)

Equipment: One beanbag per child.

Each child will need a partner. Ask the children if they can play catch with two beanbags at once. Let the children explore the various ways to do this. Some children might decide to let one partner toss both beanbags at once. Other pairs will experiment with each partner having a beanbag, and they will both toss at the same time. If the children become too frustrated with the tossing, they can try sliding the beanbags.

Potato Hot (Group)

Equipment: One box large enough to hold all of the beanbags; one beanbag per child; one bell or buzzer.

This is a '90s version of Hot Potato, but the game is played in a reverse fashion. You start with a pile of cold potatoes, and hurry to heat them in the microwave.

1. Divide the class into four equal groups. Arrange the groups in a square formation as illustrated. Put the box in the middle of the square, and explain to the children that this will be the microwave oven. Each group has a stack of cold "potatoes" that they want to hurry and cook in the microwave.

2. The potatoes for each group should be stacked beside the first player for each team. When you give the signal, the first player picks up one potato and starts passing it down his row of players. When the potato reaches the last person in the group, that player runs and puts the potato into the microwave. Then the last player goes to the head of the line to become the first player, and everyone moves down one space. As soon as one team gets a potato in the microwave, the teacher rings a bell or a buzzer to simulate the microwave timer.

3. The game is continued until everyone gets a turn to be the first player and the last player. Leave the potatoes in the microwave as the children put them there. (This is a good way to collect all of the beanbags at the end of a class.) This game could be played using just four beanbags, with each group using their own beanbag over and over again.

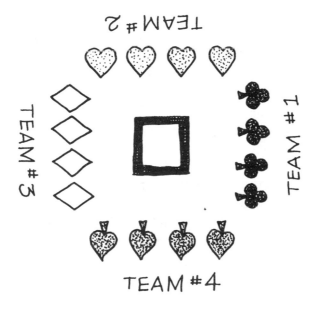

SET UP FOR 'POTATO HOT'

LESSON 5

Jumping Jacks, Jumping Jills (Equipment Activity)

Equipment: One beanbag per child.

Hold the beanbag between your feet. Jump into the air while bending your knees, so that your feet come up under you. While still in the air grab the beanbag from between your feet.

Quick Change (Warm-up, with partners)

Equipment: One beanbag for every two children.

This is a very vigorous activity, so the children can be in pairs. Designate one of the players to go first; this player will be called the "runner." The runners should all line up side by side and put their beanbag down in front of them. The partners should also be lined up side by side, 10 feet to 15 feet straight across from the runners. The partners are actually going to be used as spot markers by lying down on their backs, with their feet pointed towards the runners.

When the teacher gives the signal, the runners run across to their partners, touch the partners' toes, and run back to touch the beanbag. Let the children rest for 5 to 10 seconds, and then have them run again. Do four or five repetitions; then have the partners change jobs. If the children are not too tired, give them a second turn to run.

Get a Grip (Individuals)

Equipment: One beanbag per child.

Talk with the children about using parts of their bodies other than their hands to hold the beanbags. Emphasize that they will be holding the beanbags, not balancing them. Let the children explore, and have them share what they discover. The children can hold the beanbag:

1. under the arm,
2. in the crook of the elbow,
3. under the chin,
4. behind the knee,
5. between the elbows,
6. between the knees, and so on.

After the children have explored various ways of holding the beanbags, challenge them to move about the room while holding the beanbags. The children will discover that the way in which they are holding the beanbags may dictate the way they can move.

1. Ask the children if they always have to stay standing, or if they might move while staying low.

2. *Can you hold the beanbag differently if you are on your tummy or your back?*

3. *Do you always have to move forward, or can you sometimes move sideways, sometimes backwards?*

Up, Down, and Move Around (Individuals)

Equipment: One beanbag per child.

Review the various levels with the children. If they hold the beanbag above their shoulders, they are holding it in the high level; by their tummy is the medium level; lower than their knees is the low level.

HIGH   MEDIUM   LOW

As the teacher calls out the levels, the children hold the beanbag at that level. As the children become familiar with the levels, call out the levels faster.

Challenge the children to hold the beanbag at a certain level and move while doing so. Can they change directions?

1. *Can you hold the beanbag at a medium level and move backwards?*

2. *Can you hold the beanbag at a low level and move slowly?*

3. *Can you hold the beanbag at a high level and move sideways?*

4. *Can you hold the beanbag behind your back at a low level? How can you move?*

5. *Can you hold the beanbag at a medium level and gallop?*

6. *Can you hold the beanbag at a high level and tiptoe?*

Talented Tosses (Partners)

Equipment: One beanbag for every two children.

Let the children warm up by playing catch with the beanbag. Ask the children if there is some special or fancy way they can toss the beanbag to each other. Point out all of the terrific things you will see:

1. *Tossing backwards over your head.*
2. *Tossing sideways over your head. Can you toss sideways with your other hand too?*
3. *Tossing under your leg.*
4. *Tossing backwards through your legs.*
5. *Tossing behind your back.* Just *trying* is success!

Double Carry (Partners)

Equipment: One beanbag for every two children.

Partners should try to carry one beanbag together. The first response will be for both of the children to hold the beanbag with their hands. Encourage the children to find other ways to carry the beanbags between them while moving about the room. The children will be very creative; they will carry the beanbags:

1. Between their heads
2. Between their bottoms,
3. Between their sides (hips),
4. Between their knees,
5. Between their elbows, and so on.

Hold This! (Group)

Equipment: One beanbag per child; space markers or tape to mark a
line at each end of the room.

1. *It's great to have friends! Friends can help you in so many ways. Have you ever had a friend help you when your hands were full and you just couldn't carry another thing?* While you are speaking, pick up beanbags one by one until your arms are full of beanbags!
2. Divide the children into groups of five or six children each. Each group should line up one behind the other at one end of the room. Each group should have as many beanbags as there are children. The beanbags for each group should be in a stack on the line across the room.
3. When you give the signal, player 1 from each group runs to the other end of the room, picks up one beanbag, and carries it back to player 2. Player 1 goes to the end of the line.

4. Player 2 carries the beanbag with him across the room, picks up a second beanbag, and carries both beanbags back to player 3. Player 2 goes to the end of the line.

5. Player 3 carries both beanbags with her to the stack of beanbags, picks up still another beanbag, and carries all three bags back to player 4 (and so on.).

6. The game continues until all of the beanbags have been moved across the room. The last player will really have her hands full! If a beanbag is dropped, the player keeps running, but the beanbag is put back into the original pile to be picked up by the next player.

7. The children may enjoy a real challenge. Double the number of beanbags in each stack. Each person still picks up one beanbag at a time, but the children will need to keep taking turns until all of the beanbags have been moved across the room.

Small Balls and Buckets

INTRODUCTION

The small balls the author uses for the following activities are very soft rubber balls available at retail discount or toy stores. The balls have a 3½-inch diameter. These are not solid rubber balls, but are hollow in the center. The hollow balls are preferable for preschool use as they are lighter in weight and softer than the solid rubber balls. These balls are frequently designed to look like miniature soccer balls or basketballs.

The buckets are actually 5-quart ice cream pails with the metal handles removed. The smaller half-gallon frozen yogurt (for the really health conscious) or ice cream containers also work very well for the following lessons.

95

LESSON 1

Toss and Catch (Equipment Activity)

Equipment: One small ball per child.

As you hand out the balls, ask the children if they think they can toss and catch the ball by themselves. Many children will choose to simply toss the ball as high as they can and will never concern themselves with catching the ball. Let them explore freely for a bit. When you are ready for the children to really focus on catching the ball, then show them how you will toss the ball softly so you can catch it. Call out the names of the children who you see catching the ball. (Be generous, also, with calling out the names of those who "almost" catch the ball. Encourage others to "try again," and that should take care of nearly everyone in the class.)

Magic Passing (Warm-up)

Equipment: One small ball per child.

It is fun for you to show your magic tricks using three balls at one time. Then you can show the children how to do the tricks using just one ball.

Start by holding three balls in your left hand. (The terms left and right are only significant in that they make it easier to describe the trick.) Tell the children to watch carefully. Quickly put both hands behind your back, putting one ball in your right hand. (Special magic words of your choosing may accompany this trick.) Then quickly bring both of your hands out to the front again, showing the children that you now have two balls in one hand, and one ball in the other hand. Continue until you have all of the balls in your right hand.

Some of the children will soon point out that you are only switching the balls behind your back. Ask them if they would like to try. Other children may need to have you turn your back to them so they can actually see the "switch." Have the children try to switch the ball rapidly from one hand to the other behind their backs.

The next step, then, is for the children to switch the ball to the other hand behind their back, then to bring the ball around to their front, and switch hands again. In this manner, the ball should move rapidly around the child's waist.

Ask the children to stop. Slowly go in the opposite direction and challenge the children to do so. Going in the opposite direction can be very confusing for some children, so you should again turn your back to the children to demonstrate the switching of hands.

Challenge the children to make the ball go quickly around their ankles. Remember to try the opposite direction.

If you go very slowly, most children can learn the "Figure Eight" drill. *Stand with your feet wide. Make the ball go through your legs from the front and grab the ball with your other hand. Keep the ball in your other hand and again make it go through your legs from the front. Grab the ball with your first hand. It's very simple. Just keep putting the ball through your legs from the front and grabbing it with your free hand.*

It is difficult for most children to see how this makes the numeral 8. Since we started by doing magic, why not call this "Magic Passing." After all, it is rather magical. The ball starts in front in one hand, and it ends up in back of you in the other hand.

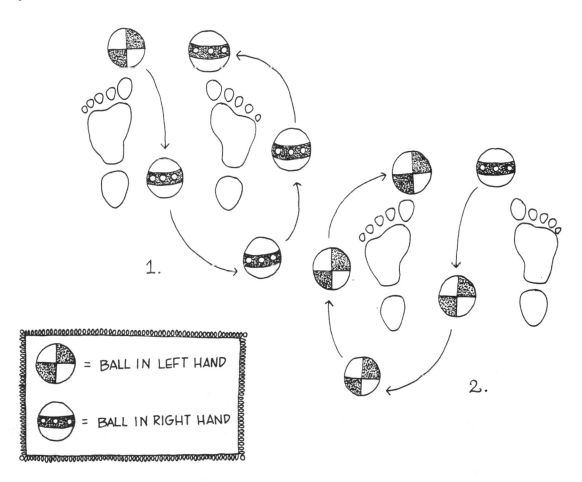

= BALL IN LEFT HAND

= BALL IN RIGHT HAND

Meatballs (Individuals)

Equipment: One small ball per child, and one flying disk (or plastic lid, or plastic spot).

1. Let the children try tossing and catching the ball, but this time challenge them to stand on their spots while they toss and catch. Remind them to try tossing with the other hand sometimes.
2. Encourage the children to try bouncing the ball and catching it.
3. Challenge the children to carry the ball on the "plate" without dropping the ball, especially since these are the "meatballs" they are having for

lunch. (The flying disks have the advantage of having an edge so the ball won't roll off as easily. The spots have the advantage that you can actually roll them up around the ball (like a hot dog bun).

4. *Put the spot on your head; put the ball on top of the spot; move about the room while holding the ball on your head.*

5. *Put the ball on top of your head; put the spot on top of the ball; move about the room while holding the spot.*

6. *Put the ball on the floor with the spot on top of it. Hold the edges of the spot and move it so you can feel the ball rolling around underneath it.*

7. *Put the ball on the floor. Hold the spot on its edge, and use the spot to push the ball around the floor.*

Tosses for Two (Partners)

Equipment: One small ball for every two children.

Assign partners and then ask the partners to play catch with one another. Show the children how to open their hands with their palms up so they are ready to catch the ball. Encourage the children to throw the ball with their palms up, also: this will be a softer underhand toss.

There are those who will have difficulty tossing and catching. They may decide just to sit down and roll the ball back and forth to one another.

Slide and Catch (Group)

Equipment: One small ball per child; one preschool climber with a slide.

This is one of the very few games in this book in which the children need to stand in line to wait for a turn. But the line moves fast, and the game is so much fun that the children don't seem to mind the wait.

The nature of this activity depends to a great degree upon the configuration of your climber. You should stand near the slide, however. Have the children take turns pushing the ball to you through an opening in the climber. Each child should follow his own ball, either climbing through an opening in the climber, going over the top of the climber, or whatever. He then slides down the slide. As soon as he is at the bottom of the slide, you roll the ball down the slide to him. He then goes to the end of the line with his own ball.

An option is to let each child roll his own ball down the slide. He then gets the added fun of chasing the ball across the room.

Speedy Ball (Group)

Equipment: One small ball per child.

The children need to sit in a closed circle. This means that each child is sitting with her legs wide apart and her feet touching the feet of the person on each side of her. Each child should start with a ball in front of her.

When the teacher gives the signal to start, the children roll the balls across the circle to each other. Keep rolling the balls as quickly as possible until the "Stop" signal is given.

Advise the children to roll the balls and not to throw them. Also point out that if a ball does go out of the circle to just let it go and not to chase it. If someone gets up to chase a ball, that will make a big hole in the circle and even more balls will get out.

LESSON 2

Behind the Back (Equipment Activity)

Equipment: One small ball per child.

As you hand out the equipment, ask the children to practice the magic trick of making the ball change hands behind their backs. Encourage the children to make up their own special magic words to accompany their trick.

Squeezies (Warm-up)

Equipment: One small ball per child.

1. *Hold the ball overhead in one hand and squeeze the ball as hard as you can. See if you can "squish" the ball. Then try the other hand.*
2. *Hold the ball under your arm (armpit) and squeeze. Be sure to try the other arm, too.*
3. *Put the ball between your bony knees and squeeze.*
4. *Put the ball between your forearm and upper arm (make "Popeye" muscles) and squeeze. Give your other arm a turn.*
5. *Put the ball under your chin and squeeze.*

Hold It! (Individuals)

Equipment: One small ball per child.

1. *Hold the ball between your knees and jump about the room.*
2. *Stand up. Hold the ball under your chin and try to drop the ball into your hands.*
3. *Lie on your back. Put both feet up in the air. Hold the ball between your feet and try to drop it into your hands.*
4. *Stand up. Hold the ball between your feet and try to jump about the room.*
5. *Where else can you hold the ball and still move about the room?*
   - *Under your chin and move backwards?*
   - *Under your arm and run?*
   - *Between your shoulder and cheek and move sideways? Try the other shoulder and move sideways in the other direction.*
6. *Sit down. Hold the ball between your feet and scoot across the floor.*

Wall Ball (Individuals)

Equipment: One small ball per child.
Each child should sit down facing the wall.

1. *Roll the ball against the wall and it will come back to you. Then, either sitting or standing, toss the ball against the wall and catch it when it comes back to you.*

2. *If you throw the ball hard, will it come back hard and fast? You bet it will! If you toss the ball softly, will it come back softly? Try it and see!*

Toss to My Partner (Partners)

Equipment: One small ball for every two children.

One person needs to lie on his back with his feet in the air, holding the ball with his feet. His partner stands behind him. He tries to toss the ball with his feet to his partner behind him. The partners should trade jobs after a designated number of turns.

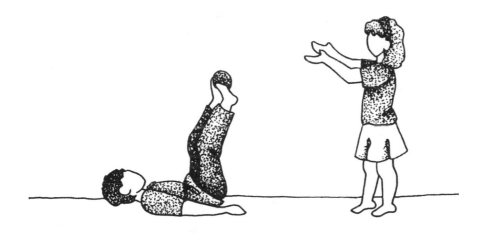

The partners should find other special ways to toss the ball to each other. Some suggestions follow:

1. *Stand up and toss the ball backwards over your head.*
2. *Stand up and bend over. Then toss the ball through your legs.*
3. *Toss the ball underneath one leg.*
4. *Bounce the ball to your partner.*

Throw and Go (Group)

Equipment: One small ball per child.

The children should line up side by side. Each child should have a ball. When you give the signal, the children should, all at the same time, throw the balls as far forward as they possibly can. The children wait for a signal and then run to find a ball.

If the balls are all marked differently (letters or numbers can be used for older children), the children should be instructed to run and find their own ball.

The children just enjoy seeing all of the balls flying at once and then chasing after them. This activity is definitely not intended to be a competition to see who can throw the farthest.

To vary the game, have the children throw the ball with their other hand. Or have them throw the ball backwards over their heads or backwards through their legs.

Tunnel Ball (Group)

Equipment: One small ball per child; one tunnel through which the children can crawl; one hula hoop.

The children line up at one end of the tunnel. They can take turns rolling their ball through the tunnel and then crawling after it.

For variation, lay a hula hoop on the floor at the far end of the tunnel. The challenge is to see if the ball can be rolled so it will stop inside the hula hoop.

The activity can become more complex if you assign a variety of tasks for the children to perform after they retrieve their ball at the far end of the tunnel. For example, challenge the children to retrieve their ball, then to put the ball between their feet and jump back to the end of the line.

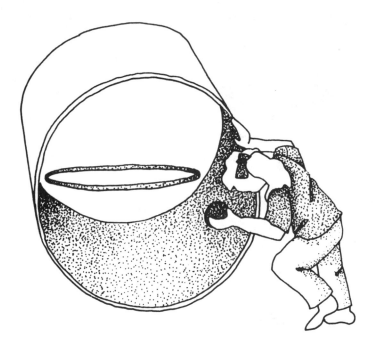

LESSON 3

Hold It 1-2-3 (Equipment Activity)

Equipment: One small ball per child.

Explore different ways to hold the ball. Hold the ball one way, such as under your chin, count to three, and find another way to hold the ball. *How many ways can you find to hold the ball?* Take a minute to let the children share some of their terrific discoveries.

Aerobi-Ball (Warm-up)

Equipment: One small ball per child; lively music source.

1. *Sit down with feet wide apart. Quickly roll the ball from one foot to the other.*

2. *Hold the ball in one hand and make large arm circles with that arm. Go in the other direction. Switch the ball to the other hand and continue with arm circles.*

3. *Sit down with your feet flat and your knees up. Hold the ball between your feet. Put your hands on the floor to help balance yourself. While still holding the ball with your feet, quickly move your feet in close to your body and then straight out in front of you.*

1.   2.

4. *Stand up with your feet wide apart. Roll the ball back and forth from one foot to the other. Speed it up!*

5. *Hold the ball with two hands. Raise your arms straight up and bring them straight down (in a chopping motion). Continue for several repetitions.*

6. *Sit down with your feet flat and your knees up. This time hold the ball between your knees. Keep your knees up, and roll your knees from side to side, getting your knees as close to the floor as possible.*

Stop and Touch (Individuals)

Equipment: One small ball per child.

1. *Put the ball on the floor. Try to gently push the ball with your feet. On the stop signal, gently put your toe on the ball. Be sure not to stand on the ball! Repeat several times, and sometimes use your other foot.*
2. *Now when you hear the stop signal, put some other part of your body on the ball.* When you first start this, you may want to say, "Stop," and then name a body part.

To further challenge the children, name the body part to use before they start moving about the room. This will require that the children remember what part to use. Another option is to simply give the children a free choice as to what body part to put on the ball.

Drop and Bump (Individuals)

Equipment: One small ball per child.

1. *Drop the ball on your head, and jump up to bump the ball with your head. Try to use other body parts to bump the ball.*
2. *Lift your knee; drop the ball on your knee and bump it up with your knee. Use the other knee, too.*
3. *Can you bump the ball with your chest?*
4. *Stick your elbow out to the side, like a wing. Try to drop the ball onto your elbow and bump it up with your elbow.*
5. *Can you bump the ball up with your shoulder?*
6. *Can you put the ball behind you and bump it with your bottom?*

Goal Kicks (Partners)

Equipment: One small ball for every two children; one milk jug or plastic bowling pin per child.

1. Two children will share one ball and two milk jugs. Show the children how to set the milk jugs up so there is some space between them. Explain that this is called a "goal," like football goalposts or a soccer goal.
2. Instruct the partners to stand across from one another, with the "goal" between them. The partners should kick the ball back and forth to each other, trying to kick the ball through the goal. As the children play, they will experiment with how much space to leave between the milk jugs.
3. The partners will now take turns. One person will rest, and the other will be the mover. The mover will push the ball along the floor, trying

to kick the ball through each goal as he comes to it. On your signal, the mover should pick the ball up and run back to his partner so she can have a turn.

Bat the Ball (Partners)

Equipment: One small ball for every two children; one milk jug or plastic bowling pin for each child.

1. Partners should stand or sit across from one another. Each child will be holding a milk jug upside down, and the partners will share a ball.
2. The partners should put the ball on the floor and try to bat the ball back and forth on the floor.
3. Other partners may then want to try to pick the ball up and bat it to their partners. Also encourage the children to try batting the ball with the milk jug in the other hand.

Kick and Go! (Group)

Equipment: One small ball per child.

The children will need to line up side by side. Each child puts her ball on the floor in front of her. On your signal, the children kick the ball as far as possible. On the "Run" signal, the children should run after the balls. Before the children run, explain that the balls all look alike. Therefore, the children do not need to try to find "their own" ball.

The more skilled children may want to try doing a drop kick (holding the ball in front of themselves and kicking it out of their hands). The other children can continue kicking the ball as it lies on the floor. Encourage the children to try using the other foot.

Circle Bowling (Group)

Equipment: Five to ten small balls; five to ten milk jugs or plastic bowling pins.

The children need to make a large circle. Set a number of milk jugs in the center of the circle. Randomly hand out a number of small balls. The children will put the balls on the floor. The object of the game is to kick the balls at the milk jugs, trying to knock over the milk jugs. The children will take turns kicking as the balls come to them on the circle. When all of the jugs are knocked over, set them up again and start over.

There are two things to consider in deciding how many balls to use. Use enough balls so the children do not have to wait too long for a turn, but do not use so many balls that they are flying so fast and furiously as to be unsafe. Generally, use one ball for every two or three children.

The milk jugs can be set up in a close cluster in the center of the circle, or they can be set up randomly about the circle with more space between them.

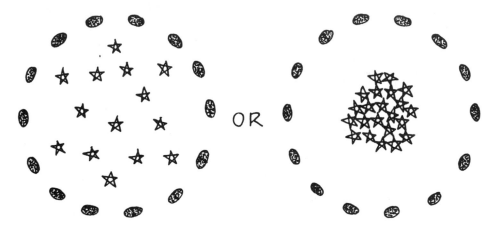

OR

⊕ = CHILD

☆ = MILK JUG

LESSON 4

Pop-ups (Equipment Activity)

Equipment: One small ball and one bucket per child.

Put the ball in the bucket. Hold the bucket with both hands. Try to toss the ball and catch it with the bucket.

Bucket of Fun (Warm-up)

Equipment: One small ball and one bucket per child.

1. *Put the ball inside the bucket, and put the bucket on the floor. Jog around the bucket. Then jog in the other direction.*
2. *Hold the bucket upside down under one arm and hold the ball in the other hand. Beat the bucket "drum" with the ball. Switch the drum to the other side.*
3. *Put the bucket upside down on your head, like a helmet. March in place, holding the ball while marching. (Another option is to have them switch the ball from hand-to-hand as they march.)*
4. *Put the bucket on the floor and stand over it with one foot on either side of it. Hold the ball with one hand and wave it vigorously. Switch the ball to the other hand.*

Bucket Toss (Individuals)

Equipment: One small ball and one bucket per child.

Put the bucket on the floor. Sit or stand away from the bucket, and try to toss the ball into the bucket. Also try tossing with the other hand. The children will feel free to experiment with the distances from the bucket.

Encourage the children to try other positions from which to toss the ball, such as backwards through the legs.

Swirl, Twirl, and Pop (Individuals)

Equipment: One small ball and one bucket per child.

1. *Put the ball into the bucket and hold the bucket with one hand. Do rapid large circles with that arm, and the ball will stay inside the bucket as it goes around.*
2. *Put the ball inside the bucket and hold the bucket with both hands. Make small, quick circles with the bucket so that the ball swirls around inside the bucket.*

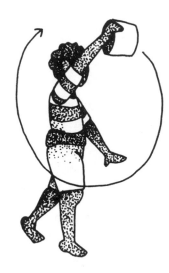

3. *Put the ball inside the bucket and hold the bucket with both hands. Make quick up-and-down motions with your arms so that the ball "pops" up and down. Sometimes do big "pops," and sometimes do little "pops."*

4. *Place the bucket on its side on the floor. Try to roll the ball into the bucket. Then place the ball on the floor. Turn the bucket on its side and try to scoop up the ball. Try it also with the bucket in the other hand.*

5. *Put the bucket on the floor. Stand over the bucket and try to drop the ball into the bucket. Use the other hand, also, to drop the ball.*

Bucket Ball (Partners)

Equipment: One bucket per child; one small ball for every two children.

The partners need to stand apart from each other so they can play catch. Challenge the children to toss the ball so their partners can catch it with their buckets. The children may want to put the bucket down while they toss the ball, or they may choose to keep hold of the bucket.

1. It won't take long for some children to decide to try to also toss the ball with the bucket.

2. Challenge the children to bounce the balls so their partners can catch them in their buckets.

3. *Try rolling the ball to each other and scooping it up with the buckets.*

Teapot (Partners)

Equipment: One bucket per child; one small ball for every two children.

Teach the children the following song:
    I'm a little teapot
    Short and stout.

Here is my handle;
Here is my spout.
When I get all steamed up;
Then I shout,
Tip me over, pour me out.

One of the partners should stand holding the bucket on her head with the ball inside the bucket. At the end of the song, she will "tip over" and pour the ball out into her partner's bucket.

Shell Game (Partners)

Equipment: One small bucket per child; one small ball for every two children.

You will first want to demonstrate this old-fashioned shell game. Turn three similar-looking buckets upside down and place a ball under one of the buckets. While talking to the children and trying to distract them, rapidly slide the buckets around into different positions. Give the children a chance to guess under which bucket the ball will be found.

You may want to demonstrate this a couple of times. Then let the partners use their two buckets to try to trick each other.

The Recycle Game (Group)

Equipment: One small bucket per child: lots of newspaper or recyclable paper wadded into paper balls; two big boxes or other containers for the paper balls.

Dump all of the paper balls into a big pile at one end of the room. The children need to stand at the far end of the room, which is where the big boxes need to be placed, also. When the teacher gives the "go" signal, the children will run with their buckets to the pile of paper, scoop up a bucketful of paper, and run back to dump the paper into one of the boxes. The children need to keep running, scooping, and dumping until all of the paper is moved to the boxes.

The game can be made a bit more competitive by dividing the class into two groups. Put one group at each end of the room, along with a box of paper balls. The object, then, is to carry buckets full of paper from your box across the room to your opponent's box. The winner is the team that can empty their box first. If you've made up the teams evenly, this could be a never-ending game.

Small Hats, Tall Hats (Group)

Equipment: One bucket per child.

1. Divide the class into groups of five or six children. The children in each group line up one behind the other at one end of the room. Each child should wear her bucket on her head—her small hat.

2. When you give the "go" signal, the first child in each line should run to his marker at the far end of the room, take his hat off and set it on the floor, and run back to his group. When the first person gets back, the second person in line takes her turn, and so on. (If the children are confused by this kind of relay, you can say "go" to start each new group of children.)

3. After all of the buckets (small hats) have been stacked up, the class is ready for the second part of the game. Each group now has one tall hat. To start the game, this tall hat is placed in front of each group. On the signal, the first player places the whole stack of buckets (the tall hat) on his head and runs to the far end of the room and back again. He then hands the tall hat to the next runner for his group. If at any time the hat falls apart, the runner simply stops, puts the hat back together, and continues to run.

Balance Beam

INTRODUCTION

The floor plan for balance beam activities in the diagram provided is suggested for two reasons. First, it shows a good progression from the easiest to the most difficult apparatus. The children can first practice on a line on the floor. They can then progress to walking on a rope that is laid straight on the floor. The next step is to a two-by-four laid directly on the floor. The children then move to a 4-inch wide elementary balance beam. The final progression, for the more daring, is to a 2-inch wide beam. The balance beams, while very low to the floor, should be set atop tumbling mats if they are available.

The second advantage of the diagrammed room arrangement is that it allows you to see the children and to be seen by the children. The children are situated so that they can all see you when you give a demonstration. (Note that the children are sitting side by side.)

When the children are working through the balance beam progression, situate yourself in the center of the room. (Note the letter *T* in the diagram.) You are then closest to the most difficult beam and thus available to help the children.

Teach the children to look straight ahead when moving on the balance beam. You might place some special markers or tape on the wall to remind the children where to look.

When helping a child who is on the balance beam, gently hold the child's waist. This helps to steady him but leaves his hands free for balance. Encourage patience. A child should not start on a piece of equipment until the person ahead of her is finished.

Lesson 1 centers around movement exploration techniques. It gives the children an opportunity to explore the balance beam and how they can move on it. The other lessons center around demonstrated techniques, thus giving all of the children a chance to try specific challenges.

The format will differ somewhat from the other series of lessons in that the needed equipment will not be listed for each activity. The suggested equipment is shown in the floor plan.

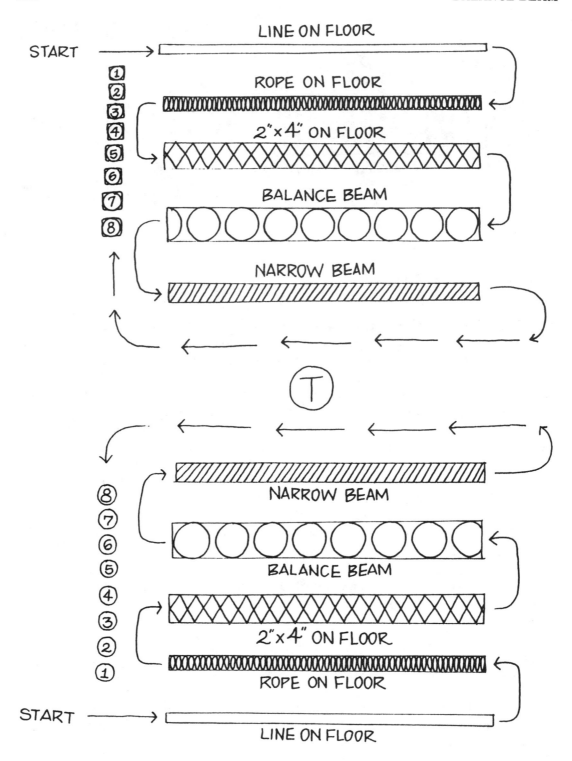

FLOOR PLAN FOR BALANCE BEAM ACTIVITIES

The following diagram shows the construction details for an elementary balance beam and a narrow balance beam. These are made entirely of two-by-fours. The elementary balance beam requires two end pieces which are constructed in the following manner: Nail two 4-inch pieces on top of a 12-inch long two-by-four. Leave approximately 4 inches of space between the 4-inch pieces so that the two-by-four beam can lie flat between the 4-inch pieces and on top of the 12-inch piece. A two-by-four is actually less than 4 inches wide, so the opening should be less than 4 inches also. This allows for a snug fit of the beam and thus prevents the beam from rocking and tilting. This makes a balance beam that is 4 inches high when completed. A higher beam can be made by nailing two 12-inch pieces together. (See diagram for details.)

The narrow balance beam is constructed in much the same way, but the opening should be slightly under 2 inches. This in turn means that the top pieces will be slightly more than 5 inches. Using two 5-inch pieces on each side will prevent the beam itself from rocking and tilting. The two-by-four will lie on its edge between the end pieces. The children will thus be walking on a beam that is slightly less than 2 inches wide.

The two-by-four which acts as the beam itself can be 6 feet to 8 feet long, depending on how you will transport and store it. It is extremely important to carefully sand all of the wood pieces to prevent splinters. It's fun to write all of the children's names on the beams using permanent markers.

ELEMENTARY BALANCE BEAM CONSTRUCTION

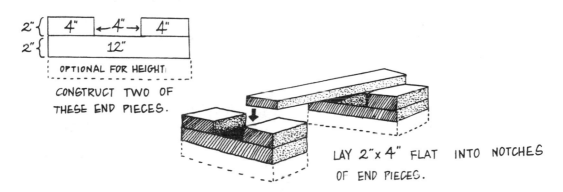

NARROW BALANCE BEAM CONSTRUCTION

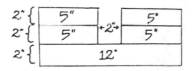

LESSON 1

Get in Shape! (Warm-up)

Equipment: Optional: lively music.

1. *Jog in place. Pick your feet up; keep your knees up high.*
2. *Sit with your legs in front of you in a V shape. Use your fingers to make the "itsy bitsy spider," and walk that spider down each leg. Go as far as you can, but don't let your leg come up off the floor. Walk the spider down each leg several times.*
3. *Raise your left arm over your head and lean far to the right.* (The children don't actually need to know left and right. Simply demonstrate the activity. Left and right is simply the easiest way for you to understand the directions.) *Raise the right arm straight up, and lean far to the left.*
4. *Hold your arms straight out to the sides. Make big arm circles. Try small circles.*
5. *Sit with your feet together in front of you. Hold your arms straight out in front. Open your arms and legs as far as you can at the same time. Repeat the opening and closing several times.*

Can You? (Individuals)

1. *Can you find a way to move forward across the balance beam?* Repeat this question three or four times, or as long as the children are still exploring.
2. *Can you find a way to move backward or sideways across the beam?* Let the children explore several ways.
3. *Can you keep your body very low while moving across the beam?*

4. *Can you move across the balance beam using your hands and your feet?*

5. *Can you move across the beam with part of your body on the balance beam and part of it on the floor?*

6. *How can you hold your arms while on the balance beam?*
   - *Above your head?*
   - *Down by your sides?*
   - *Straight out in front of you?*
   - *One up and one down?*
   - *Can you flap your arms like a bird while on the beam? Does that make it harder to stay on the beam?*

7. *Can you stop in the middle of the beam and do a trick?*
   - *Stand on one foot?*
   - *Clap behind your back?*

Two on the Beam (Partners)

1. *You and your partner find a way to move across the balance beam together.*

2. *Can you move across the balance beam without anyone going backwards?*

3. *Without using your hands, can you touch each other while moving across the beam?*

4. *One partner stays high and one stays low while moving across the balance beam. Try it again with the partners changing positions.*

5. *Can you stop in the middle and do a balancing trick with your partner?*

Giddyup! (Group)

This is an activity to remind you and the children to always use your imagination. Don't always look at things the same way. For example, a balance beam isn't just a balance beam. It also makes a terrific extra-long horse!

Each group should sit one behind the other on their horse. The children will hold the reins, bounce their feet, and ride like the wind! To ensure a lot of happy little cowpokes, you can shout out "Whoa," which is the cue for the last person on the horse to run to the front and be the lead rider. Everyone else slides one space back. (Make sure the balance beams are well sanded to prevent splinters in their "git-alongs.")

Challenge the riders to swing a lasso with one arm while riding the horse. Change and use the other arm.

LESSON 2

Zoo Moves (Warm-up)

1. *Flap your arms like a bird. Then hold them out as if you are soaring. Do giant flaps as a giant bird might do. Try small, fast flaps as a hummingbird might do.*
2. Turtle Tuck: *Lie on your back. Put your arms and legs up in the air. Then quickly pull the arms and legs in toward your tummy. Repeat several times.*
3. Cat Stretch: *Get on your hands and knees. Now arch your back like a mad cat. Then sway your back so your tummy points to the ground. Continue arching and swaying alternately. It should be a slow, gentle stretch.*
4. Giraffe Neck: *Slowly bend your neck forward, backward, and side to side.*
5. Kangaroo Jump: *Jump in place, jumping as high as you can.*
6. Snake Curl: *Lie on the floor, stretching yourself out as long as you can. Then curl up into a tight ball. Keep stretching and curling.*

Balance Beam Walks (Individuals)

1. *Warm up by walking forward on the balance beam. Remember to look straight ahead.*
2. *Walk backwards by putting one foot behind the other. Watch for the back end of the balance beam.*
3. *Try moving sideways on the balance beam. Some children will move with a step-together movement.*
4. *Can you move sideways by crossing one foot over the other?*
5. *Can you move across the beam on your tiptoes?*

Fancy Prancing

1. *Take a step. Then slide your back foot up to meet the other foot. Step and slide all the way across the balance beam. Remember to look straight ahead.*
2. *Let's try going a little faster. Try galloping across the balance beam.*
3. *Can you move across the beam taking very fancy high steps?*
4. *Try taking very long, giant steps. How many steps does it take you to get across the balance beam?*

Two Beam or Not Two Beam (Partners)

1. *You and your partner walk to the center of the beam, stop in the middle and stand on one foot. Partners may walk one behind the other or side*

by side. Try it first without holding hands, and then try it holding hands or waists. Also be sure to try balancing on each foot.

2. *Move to the middle of the beam, squat, and stand back up. Try it first without touching each other, and then try it holding on to one another. Try squatting while standing side by side on the beam.*

3. *Move sideways together to the middle of the beam. Hold inside hands and raise them high. One person stands still while her partner turns in a circle under their upraised arms.*

1.

2.

Follow Me (Partners)

One person is the leader, and his partner follows his movements across the balance beam. Encourage the children to do fancy movements with their arms or to take fancy steps. Give each partner a turn to be the leader.

Balancing Train (Group)

Equipment: Tumbling mats under and around the balance beams are recommended.

Start with groups of four or five children. With success, the size of the group can be increased.

The children form a train by standing one behind the other and holding each others' waists. By taking small steps, the train chug-chug-chugs across the beam. Challenge the children to move the train backwards.

Chorus Line (Group)

Equipment: Tumbling mats under and around the balance beams are recommended.

1. Start with groups of four or five children. The children stand side by side on the balance beam without touching one another. Challenge the children to balance on one foot. Then try the other foot. Repeat the challenges with all of the children holding hands.

2. Line up the entire class side by side on the floor. The children hold hands. Challenge the children to stand on one foot and then the other foot. Ask the children if they can all jump up and down together.

3. Show the children how to jump and kick one leg out and then the other leg. Challenge the whole group to do this together while holding hands. The children can be very successful with this if they keep their legs straight—no fancy knee bends and kicks. And they certainly will not be in step. The challenge for them will simply be to keep holding hands while all of them are moving.

LESSON 3

Jumping Legs, Dancing Arms (Warm-up)

Equipment: Optional: lively music.
The children are in scattered formation (not on beams).

1. Individuals do the Chorus Line kick, alternately kicking feet out in front.
2. *Raise both arms up in the air, fingers spread; bring both arms down to your chest. Repeat several times.*
3. *Jumping Jack feet, jumping, alternately moving feet together and then apart.*
4. *Hold arms out to sides, then bring them together straight out in front. Repeat several times.*
5. *Jump, alternately crossing feet and moving feet wide apart. Repeat several times.*
6. *Hold arms out to sides, then bring them together straight out in front, crossing them over each other. Hold the arms straight even as they cross.*

Across the Beam (Individuals)

Equipment: One beanbag for each balance beam.

1. *Warm up by moving across the beam however you like. Remember to look straight ahead.*
2. *Try running across the balance beam. Is it easier if you run on tiptoes?*
3. *Squat down and try moving across the beam, walking like a duck. Remember to look straight ahead. Keep your back straight and your seat down; then you'll be a tall, proud duck!*
4. *Can you walk on your hands and feet to move across the balance beam? Remember to look straight ahead. Can you go backwards this way?*
5. *How can you move across the balance beam if you move with one foot on the beam and one foot on the floor? Now put the other foot on the beam and your other foot on the floor. Do you always have to move forward? Do you always have to stand up high?*
6. *Can you move across the balance beam while balancing a beanbag on your head? Where else can you balance the beanbag while moving on the balance beam? Can you move sideways or backwards while balancing the beanbag? Can you balance more than one beanbag and move across the beam?*

Balancing Stunts (Individuals)

After the teacher demonstrates these balancing stunts, the children may all want to practice them together on the floor before getting on the balance beams. (Do not practice these stunts on the ropes, as that would be most uncomfortable.)

For all of the stunts, the children should walk to the center of the balance beam, perform the stunt, and then walk to the end of the beam. Whenever the children use their hands on the beam they should grasp the edges of the beam, with thumbs on top and fingers on the bottom of the beam.

It would be ideal to have tumbling mats under and around the balance beams.

V-Sit

1. *Sit on the beam. Put your hands behind you and hold on to the beam. Keep your legs straight as you raise them together off the balance beam. Raise your legs until your legs and your body together make the shape of the letter* V.

2. *Try to hold that position while letting go of the beam and holding your arms out to the side.*

Foot and Knee Balance

1. *Stand on the beam with one foot in front of the other. Take a giant step forward with the front foot.*

2. *Bend your knees until your back knee is resting on the balance beam. Keep your back straight—be tall! Hold your arms straight out to the side.*

3. *Can you try this with the other foot in front?*

Front Support

1. *Start by standing in the center of the balance beam. Reach down and grasp the beam with both hands. While still holding onto the beam, slowly walk your feet backwards until your legs and body make a straight line. Your bottom should not be sticking up in the air. Now lift your head and look straight forward.*

2. *Can you hold this position and pick up one foot? Put your foot back down and pick up one hand.*

Stork Stand

1. *Face forward on the balance beam. Lift one foot off the beam and hold that free foot next to your knee. Try this while balancing on the other leg.*
2. *Can you do the Stork Stand while raising both arms straight over your head?*

Rear Support

Sit on the balance beam with your legs straight in front of you. Reach behind you and grasp the edges of the beam. Raise your seat off the balance beam and push your tummy up until your body and your legs make a straight line.

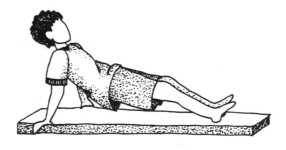

Balancing Under and Over (Partners)

Equipment: One wand for every two people. (The wands can be broomsticks or plastic golf tubes. Rubber band ropes could also be substituted if there are groups of three children, with two of the children holding the rope across the balance beam.)

1. One partner stands beside the balance beam and holds the wand across the beam. He needs to hold it high enough for his partner to walk under while on the beam. With each trip across the balance beam the partner will lower the wand. Continue until the walker can no longer get under the wand and then trade jobs.

2. Partners trade back to their original jobs, but this time the holding partner will start by holding the wand low enough for his partner to step over the wand. He gradually raises the wand higher with each trip across the beam until the walker can no longer step over the wand. Then trade jobs again!

Pick 'Em Up (Partners)

Equipment: One beanbag for every two people.

1. One partner places the beanbag somewhere on the balance beam. Her partner has to walk on the beam, squat, pick up the beanbag, then stand up and walk to the end of the balance beam. Then trade jobs.

2. Try it again with the partner placing the beanbag on the *floor* near the balance beam. Her partner attempts to squat down and retrieve the beanbag without losing his balance.

Scarecrow Balance (Group)

Equipment: Several beanbags for each group.

The groups can be any size, as only two people at a time will take a turn with this activity. This is done as a group activity simply so the children can share the beanbags.

One person stands sideways on the center of the balance beam, posing like a scarecrow with arms straight out and feet wide apart. One or two of the other children start placing bean bags on the scarecrow's arms, head, shoulders, etc. See how many beanbags the scarecrow can balance at one time. The scarecrow then goes to the end of the line.

Balance and Pass (Group)

Equipment: Several beanbags per group.

Each group lines up one behind the other on a balance beam. Start with a beanbag at the front of the line. Each child in turn passes the beanbag over her head to the person behind her. The game can be continued in one of two ways: Only one beanbag can be used, in which case the last person in line gets off the balance beam, walks to the front of the line, and starts passing the beanbag again. Or, the leader can have a whole stack of beanbags and keeps passing beanbags one at a time until all of the beanbags are at the end of the line.

This game can also be played with the children standing side by side.

Stunts and Tumbling

INTRODUCTION

The diagram on the next page shows a possible arrangement for the tumbling mats. The emphasis of the arrangement is *visibility*. That is, all the children can see you when you demonstrate. And, you can see all of the children because they are not hidden behind one another in lines. Also, the children are situated so they can watch one another, and that allows them to be more patient if they have to wait for a turn.

It would be even more helpful to use colored spots on the floor to designate waiting spots for the children. It is a given, that if children wait alongside of tumbling mats they always end up with their arms, legs, heads, or whole bodies on the mats while someone else is trying to work on the mat. So move the spots well back from the mats and point out to the children the importance of staying back.

Safety must be taught first when the children are introduced to stunts and tumbling. There may be room for two or three children to be on the mat at the same time if they are doing static stunts, stunts where they do not move from one end of the mat to the other. In this case, the children need to learn to position themselves on the mat so that they make the best use of the "safe space." For example, it is likely that children doing the V-sit will roll backwards. Before doing the V-sit, they should look behind them and make sure there is empty mat space ("safe space"). When doing the Donkey Kick, the children are likely to fall or roll forward, so there must be safe space in front of them. The children will need guidance to become aware of safe space, but it is an excellent way to help the children develop kinesthetic awareness.

If the children are doing moving stunts, where they actually move from one end of the mat to the other, they will need to take turns. Caution the children

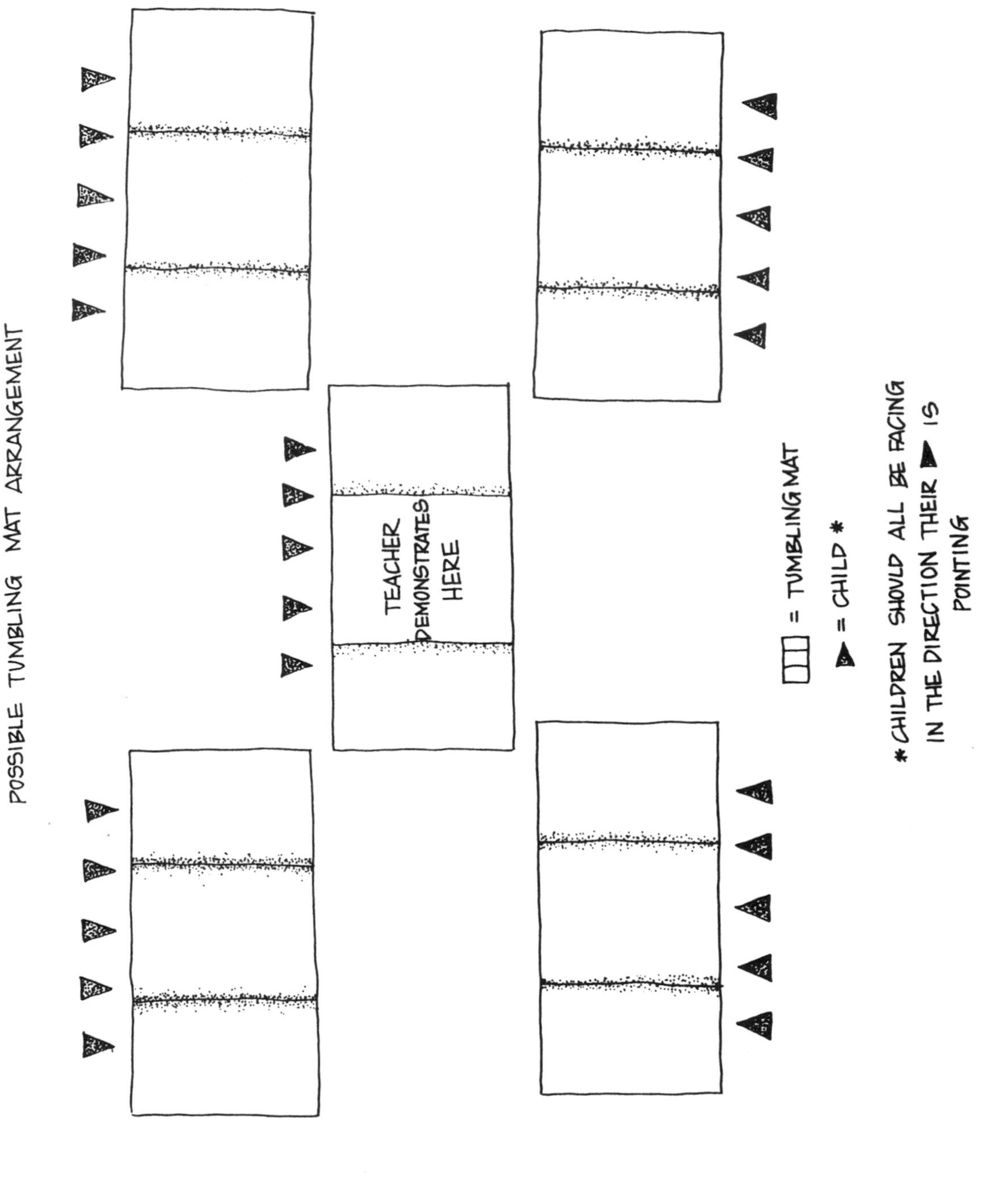

POSSIBLE TUMBLING MAT ARRANGEMENT

TEACHER
DEMONSTRATES
HERE

☐ = TUMBLING MAT

▲ = CHILD *

* CHILDREN SHOULD ALL BE FACING
IN THE DIRECTION THEIR ▶ IS
POINTING

to wait for the person in front to be finished and off the mat before starting their own stunt. (Remember, it is usually easier for the children to wait if they are alongside of the mat.) For their safety and that of the performer the children need to learn to stay out of the way of the performer.

You should demonstrate at the center mat. You may also have children demonstrate, but do so at the center mat. Do the demonstration twice, once facing each end of the room.

Most preschool establishments have safety mats under their climbers. Perhaps it will also be possible to borrow mats from local schools or YMCAs for a short period of time. Preschools, daycare centers, and early childhood organizations could purchase equipment together and rotate it among the centers.

In all of the lessons involving partners, the partners should be of approximately equal size unless otherwise stated.

This section is the most demanding in that it requires the most specific movements. In the case of stunts and tumbling, there are right and wrong ways to perform the maneuvers. Every attempt has been made to point out key phrases to help the children move correctly. If you do not feel confident in teaching stunts and tumbling, you might find local junior high school, high school, college, or gymnastic club athletes to volunteer a couple of hours of their time. What heroes they would be to the preschoolers!

LESSON 1

Jumping Beings (Warm-up)

Equipment: Tumbling mat space for everyone, with two or three children sharing a mat.

1. *Jump up and down on a mat. Can you jump up and down like a bouncing ball? How does the mat feel under your feet?*
2. *Lie on your back. Put your arms above your head and roll from side to side. Don't roll all the way over.*
3. *Stand with your feet wide apart. Bend your knees and squat part-way down—pretend you are sitting in a chair. Stand up again. Repeat the Chair Sit several times. Can you "sit" and cross one leg over the other?*
4. *Get on your hands and knees. On the signal,* **push** *your hands down into the mat, trying to squish the mat. Relax and then go again on the signal.*

Log Roll (Individuals)

Equipment for Individual Challenges: Tumbling mat space for everyone. (This applies to all the individual challenges in Lesson 1.)

The children line up at one end of the mat. They will take turns doing the roll and should wait until the person ahead of them is finished before taking their turn.

1. *Lie down across the width of the mat with your hands and head pointing toward one side of the mat. Try to roll in a straight line to the other end of the mat. When finished, go to the end of your line.*
2. *Repeat the Log Roll, but this time have your hands and head toward the other side of the mat. This allows the children to practice rolling in the other direction.*

V-Sit (Individuals)

1. *Sit on the mat with your legs in front of you. Make sure there is free space behind you. Bend your knees and slide your feet in close so you can grab hold of your toes. Keeping a hold of your toes, raise your legs off the mat so your legs and body make the shape of the letter* V. *Keep sitting up!* The tendency will be to roll back onto their backs.
2. *Can you still hold your legs up if you take your hands away and hold your arms out to the side?*

Half Turn (Individuals)

1. *Stand on the mat with your feet shoulder width apart. Jump up and turn half way around. Land lightly on both feet, standing tall. Use your arms to help you turn, but try to stand very still when you land, with your arms down at your sides.* Limit the children to only three or four attempts or they will become dizzy.

2. *Can you turn in the other direction?*

Rocking Chair (Individuals)

1. *Lie on your tummy on the mat across the width of the mat, with your head pointing toward one side of the mat. Bend your knees, arch your back, and reach back to grasp your feet with your hands.*

2. *Pull hard on your feet, and lift your head and shoulders off the mat. Rock your body back and forth from your chest to your thighs.*

Tipsy Turtle (Individuals)

Roll over on your back. Pull your knees up to your chest, and wrap your arms around your knees. Now you're like a turtle on its back. Rock back and forth on your back. This is a great activity to follow the Rocking Chair—it gets the kinks out.

Heel Clicks (Individuals)

1. *Stand on the mat with your feet together. Quickly raise one leg out to the side and jump your other foot up to meet it, clicking your heels together.*

2. *Repeat the activity, starting with the other leg.*

Seal Balances (Individuals)

1. *Lie on your tummy across the width of the mat. Hold your body up off the mat with your hands and feet. Keep your seat down so your body is in a straight line.*

2. *Pick one foot up so your are balancing on two hands and one foot. Keep your body straight! Can you change feet and still keep your balance?*

3. *Start again on both hands and both feet. Pick up one hand so you are balancing on one hand and two feet. Then switch hands.*

4. *Can you pick up one hand and one leg and still balance? Can you pick up the hand and leg on the same side of your body?*

Shoulder Rest (Individuals)

Lie on your back across the width of the mat. Roll back until your hips are above your head. Try to get as much of your back off the mat as you can, so you are resting on your shoulders. Put your elbows on the mat, and use your hands to help hold your hips up. Point your feet straight up to the ceiling.

Note in All Partner Challenges: Remind the students that when they are working with partners, they are responsible for their partner's safety.

Wring the Dishcloth (Partners)

Equipment: This can be done on the floor; no mats are needed.

Partners stand facing each other and hold hands. *Raise one pair of arms, turn together under the raised arms, and end in a back-to-back position while still holding hands. Raise the other pair of arms and turn under the newly raised arms to end facing your partner.*

It is easier to learn this if it is taught in two steps. However, once the students learn which arms to raise and to turn under the raised arms, they will be able to Wring the Dishcloth in one continuous motion.

1.

BOTH TURN UNDER
RAISED ARMS...

2.

UNTIL PARTNERS ARE BACK TO
BACK. LOWER RAISED ARMS
& RAISE OTHER SET OF ARMS.

Double Stand (Partners)

Equipment: Mat for each set of partners.

Partners sit back-to-back and lock elbows with each other. The partners should try to stand up together while keeping their elbows locked together. Coach them to bend their knees and brace their feet flat on the floor. It is also helpful to push against each other's backs.

Leap Frog (Partners)

Equipment: Mats are *not* needed; this can be done safely on the floor.

One child crouches on his knees, with his head tucked down and his arms over his head for protection. This child is the "rock" over which the "frog" is leaping. The frog places her hands on the bottom child's shoulders and spreads her legs wide as she jumps over the rock. The frog should land on her feet and immediately crouch down to become the rock. The rock then stands up and becomes the leaping frog.

Archway (Partners)

Equipment: Mat for each set of partners.

The partners lie down on their backs along the length of the mat. Their heads should be in the center of the mat, and each partner's feet point to an opposite end of the mat.

The partners slide a little apart so their heads are not touching. Each partner does a Shoulder Rest. Their feet touch in the air, forming an archway.

Coach the children to place their elbows on the mat, hold their hips up with their hands, and keep their legs straight.

Mat Tag (Group)

Equipment: Tumbling mats scattered about the room or left in the basic four-corner formation.

This is a basic game of tag, with one person being "It." The tumbling mats are all bases where the children can go to be safe from It. However, when a child goes to a tumbling mat, she must immediately count to five (or ten) and then leave that mat immediately. Every child tagged joins "It" as a tagger. The game is played until everyone is tagged.

LESSON 2

Jogging (Warm-up)

Equipment: No equipment is needed, but it would be helpful to have the mats already arranged in the four-corner formation.

Lead the children in jogging around the room, and around the outside of the tumbling mats.

Heel Slap (Individuals)

Equipment: Mats in the four-corner formation.

*Stand with your feet shoulder-width apart. Jump high in the air and bend your knees so your heels come up **behind** you and to the side near your hips. Slap your heels with your hands.*

Full Turn (Individuals)

Equipment: Mats.

1. *Stand on the mat with your feet shoulder-width apart. Try to jump high and turn all the way around, landing again on your feet. Twist your body to help get yourself around. Try to land very still, with your arms down at your sides.*

2. *Only try this three or four times in each direction. Too many turns will make you dizzy.*

Mad Cat (Individuals)

Equipment: No tumbling mats are needed, as this can be done safely on the floor.

1. *With your tummy towards the floor, hold yourself up on your hands and feet. Hold your body in a straight line. Keep your hands flat on the floor and walk your feet up as close to your hands as you can. The hard part is that you have to keep your legs straight! This means that you will round your back and your seat will be up in the air. You will look like a mad cat arching its back.*

2. *The next step is to keep your feet still and walk your hands forward until your body is straight again.*

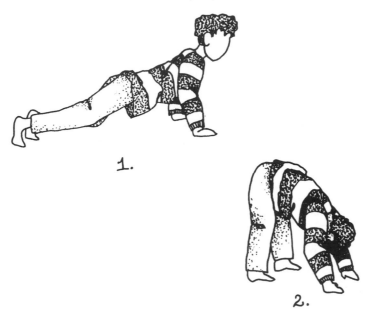

1.

2.

THEN WALK IT BACK TO #1!

Knee Walk (Individuals)

Equipment: Mats.

The children will need to take turns moving down the length of the mat. Remind them to wait until the person ahead of them is done with his turn.

*Kneel down at one end of the mat. Keep your upper body erect—do not sit on your knees. Reach back and grasp your feet or your ankles, and pull your feet up close to your seat. Lean **slightly** forward and walk on your knees. If you start to fall, let go of your feet and catch yourself with your hands.*

Donkey Kick (Individuals)

Equipment: Mats. Children may share space on the mats, but each person must have lots of free mat space in front of himself.

You have to have strong arms to do the Donkey Kick. Your arms have to hold you up. Bend over from a standing position and put your hands flat on the floor. Your seat will be in the air. Give a quick jump off both feet and kick your feet up in the air—just like a donkey!

Encourage the children to start with a small kick so they get the feel of the move. Kicking too high will cause the children to flip over forward, which is why they need mat space in front of them. Remind the children to keep their arms straight and sturdy.

Forward Roll (Individuals)

Equipment: Mats. The children can most likely share the mats when they are first learning to roll. They can be spaced evenly along the width of the mat, and there should be enough mat space in front of them to safely do one roll.

1. To get the children into the correct position for rolling, first teach them to make "frog knees." That is, they should squat with their knees opened wide. This open space is where their heads go as they start their roll.

2. *Try to put your chin on your chest so your head and shoulders are nice and round. Put your hands on the floor just in front of your knees and push with your feet. If you keep your chin tucked and your back round like a ball, you will roll over very smoothly.*

3. *Remember, when you roll you do* **not** *put your head down on the mat. Your head should just brush the mat as you roll over. When you roll over, your shoulders should land on the mat first.* The correct weight transfer for a forward roll is: feet to hands to shoulders to back.

The description above is the most technically correct way to teach a forward roll. However, because of their body builds, many preschoolers have difficulty doing a roll starting from the squat position. In this case, let them start from a standing position and simply bend straight over. They still need to keep their chins tucked and backs rounded. The weight transfer is the same.

A child who has trouble staying round may need to practice the feeling of a round back. She should lie on her back and pull her knees up, wrapping her arms around her knees. She should then pull her head and shoulders off the mat and rock back and forth. Have her try to keep her chin on her chest while rocking.

Over the Fence (Partners)

Equipment: No tumbling mats are needed; this can be done very safely on the floor.

1. Partners stand facing one another. They need to shake hands, either right to right or left to left. The partners lean down so their joined arms are lowered somewhat. (Right and left will be used to expedite the explanation.) Partner 1 swings her right leg over the joined arms so she ends up straddling the arms, with her back to Partner 2. Partner 2 then swings her left leg over the joined arms and ends up straddling the arms, with her back to Partner 1.

2. Partner 1 then continues around by swinging her left leg over the arms. Partner 2 follows by swinging her right leg over, and the partners are back in their starting positions. As the partners are swinging their legs over the "fence," it is easier if the fence is lowered.

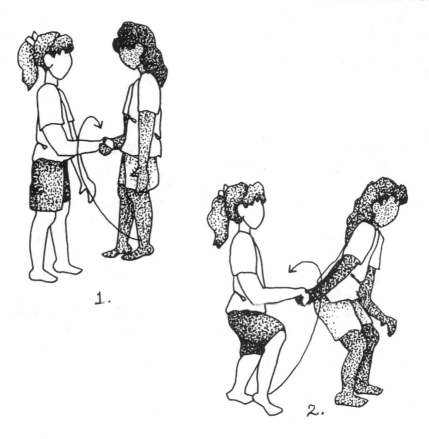

1.

2.

Two Step (Partners)

Equipment: This will be more comfortable if the children remove their shoes; mats are recommended.

The partners stand facing one another and hold on to one another's shoulders. One person (the "top") stands on the other person's (the "base") feet. It is easier if the top turns her feet outward. The base picks up her feet and walks across the mat, carrying the top with her.

If the partners are the same size, they should trade jobs to walk back across the mat.

Teeter Totter (Partners)

Equipment: Mats.

The sets of partners will need to take turns trying this on the center of the mat.

1.   Partners sit facing one another with their knees bent and their feet flat on the mat. The partners move close enough together to sit on each other's feet. One partner has his legs on the outside, and the other has his legs on the inside. They hold onto one another's shoulders.

2. As Partner 1 leans back and raises his feet off the mat, Partner 2 leans forward and brings his weight forward onto his feet. This will bring Partner 2's seat off the mat. Then Partner 2 sits down and rocks back while Partner 1 leans forward and comes up on his feet. The partners continue this teeter totter motion.

ROCK BACK & FORTH

Wheelbarrow (Partners)

Equipment: Mats.

The sets of partners will need to take turns trying this on the mat. They should start at one end of the mat.

1. One partner starts down on her hands and knees; this person is the "wheelbarrow." Her partner stands behind her, and she will move the wheelbarrow down the mat. The wheelbarrow needs to open her legs so her partner can stand between her feet. She then reaches down and picks the wheelbarrow up *by the knees*.
2. The wheelbarrow moves by walking on her hands. The back partner simply holds the legs up **by the knees** and *does not push* the wheelbarrow. The partners can change jobs when they get to the end of the mat.

Log Ride (Group)

Equipment: Depending on the size of the group, two tumbling mats may be moved end to end to provide a longer rolling surface.

A group of ten to twelve children is ideal for teaching this stunt. Starting at one end of the mat, all of the children except one lie down on their tummies across the width of the mat. Their arms are on the mat above their heads. The children need to be touching each other, with their hips lined up. There should be no empty space between the children, the "logs."

The one child who does not lie down is the rider. (Start with the smallest person in the class as the rider.) She lies down across the logs, lying on their hips. When the teacher gives the signal, the logs slowly roll together down the mat, and the rider will take a ride right across the logs. (It works best, if there is another adult, for that adult to be the lead log. She can thus keep the logs rolling slowly.)

Continue taking turns until every person gets a chance to be the rider. Position the heavier riders on the seats or legs of the logs. Use your good judgment about rider size and safety.

LESSON 3

Jumping Jacks and Jills (Warm-up)

Equipment: No equipment is needed, but it would be helpful to have the tumbling mats already arranged in the four-corner formation. Leave the teacher's mat (or the mat in the center) out of the center area. The children can all find space on the floor inside the four-corner formation.

1. *Jump up and down doing Jumping Jack feet. (Jump, alternating feet apart and feet together.)*
2. *Stand still. Alternately clap hands above your head, and bring your arms down to your sides.*
3. *Jump and bring both knees up, slapping your knees.*
4. *Stand still. Alternate putting your hands on your hips and putting your hands up in the air.*
5. *Jump and bend your legs backward, trying to kick your seat.*
6. *Stand still. Alternate holding your arms out straight and touching your shoulders.*

X-Stand (Individuals)

Equipment: As many tumbling mats as possible. One suggestion is to arrange them in the four-corner formation.

Two or three children can share the space on each mat.

1. *Stand with your feet crossed, like the letter* X. *Then cross your arms like the letter* X. *Try to carefully sit down, keeping your feet and arms crossed. Try to control your legs and your body so you don't fall over.*
2. *After sitting down, keep your feet and arms crossed. Now try to stand up. Keep your arms crossed!*

Frog Dance (Individuals)

Equipment: None.

The children can try this on the tumbling mats or on the floor. It is actually easier to do on the floor.

The children can take turns "dancing" on the mats, and then the floor.

Squat down with your knees wide apart, like a frog. Put your hands flat on the floor, between your knees. Kick one leg straight out to the side, touching the floor with that foot. Bring that leg back in and kick the other leg straight out to the side. Alternate kicking your legs out to the side. Does this look like a frog dancing?

1.

2.

Jump and Roll *(Individuals)*

Equipment: Individuals will need to perform this routine one at a time on the mats.

You or a student may demonstrate this combination of moves. *When we put some tumbling moves together, it is called a "routine." Try to do each move very carefully; be in control of your body.*

1. *Stand at one end of the mat, facing away from the mat. Jump and do a half turn so you now have the mat in front of you.*
2. *Do a forward roll.*
3. *End with an "Olympic Stand."* (The author's version of an "Olympic Stand" is: feet together and arms straight up in a *V*.)

Special Somersaults *(Individuals)*

Equipment: Individuals will need to perform this routine one at a time on the mats, but they can share the space for practicing their jumps and balances.

Show the children a variety of "fancy" jumps and let them experiment. *A "fancy" jump just means doing something different with your legs when you jump.* Some examples are:

1. *Jump and spread your legs wide apart.*
2. *Do a "split" jump, with one leg forward and one leg back.*
3. *Jump up and kick your seat.*
4. *Jump up and slap your knees.*
5. *Jump with your legs out straight in front of you and touch your toes.*

Try some fancy balances on one foot. Do something fancy with your arms or your legs:

1. *How can you make your arms look fancy?*
2. *Hold your free leg straight out in front.*
3. *Bend at the waist and hold your free leg straight back.*
4. *Hold your free foot on the knee of your balancing leg.*

Challenge the children to put three moves together into a routine: a fancy jump, followed by a forward roll, ending with a fancy balance. The teacher can demonstrate her own routine, and the children can try that first. But everyone needs to make up their own Special Somersault!

Table Stand (Partners)

Equipment: Partners will need to take turns using the mats.

This partner activity offers the chance to talk with the children about their uniqueness and about safety. *We all have our own special shape and our own special size. If you and your partner are different sizes, which of you should be the table? Which of you should stand on the table? Would it be safe to stand on a person who is smaller than you are?*

1. The "table" gets down on her hands and knees. (Preschoolers have a tendency to squat back on their knees. Be sure they are up straight on their knees.) *Keep your back straight—no bumps or dips.*
2. Before the top stands on the table, show the children where it is safe to stand. *It is safe to stand on the hips or across the shoulders, but not in the middle of the back!* Emphasize how important this is for safety. Another child may help the top balance while he steps up and stands on the hips of the table. The top should try to stand alone, with his arms out straight. The top should *step* down off the table and not jump. Jumping puts an extra strain on the table.

You may choose to be the table for those children who would not otherwise get to be the top.

Triangle (Partners)

Equipment: Mats.

One child (the "base") sits on the mat with his legs straight out in front of him. The "top" gets on her hands and knees, with her knees on either side of the base's legs, and her feet next to the base's hips.

With his fingers and thumbs pointing up, the base grabs hold under the top's ankles and lifts her legs up to his shoulders. The top needs to hold her arms stiff and straight. The top should keep her head up and look straight ahead. *Does this make a triangle shape?*

If the partners are the same size they can trade jobs.

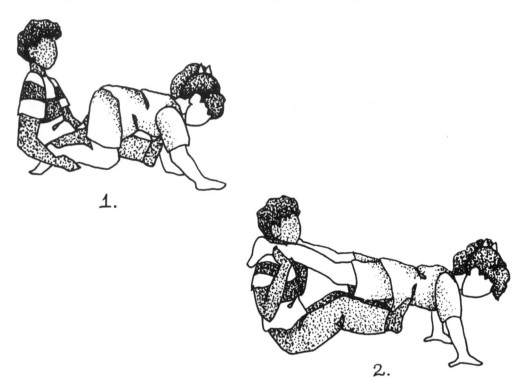

Double Shoulder Stand (Groups)

Equipment: Each group of children can stay at their tumbling mat. This is an activity for three children, so the children can take turns trying the stunt.

Emphasize the safe way for the tops to stand on the bases. There are two bases. They are in the center of the mat on their hands and knees, with the tops of their heads touching. Another child can help the top to get up onto the bases.

The top stands with one foot on the shoulders of one base and the other foot on the shoulders of the second base. The top should keep her head up and look straight ahead.

Double Table Stand (Groups)

Equipment: Mats.

This activity is nearly identical to the Double Shoulder Stand, but the two bases turn around so they are facing away from each other. There may be some space between the bases.

Another child can help the top to stand with one foot on the hips of each base.

Pyramid (Groups)

Equipment: Each group of children can stay at their tumbling mat. This is an activity for five children: three bases and two tops.

Three children are on their hands and knees, side by side in the center of the tumbling mat. They are the bases. Two children stand on the hips of the three bases. One top has one foot on the left base and one foot on the center base. The other top has one foot on the right base and one foot on the center base. The center base holds the most weight.

Remind the tops to step down carefully. Jumping down puts extra strain on the bases.

Stretch Steps and Obstacle Courses

INTRODUCTION

Your primary focus in the lessons that follow should be the challenges involving the Stretch Steps. This is because the challenges presented by the Stretch Steps will most likely be new and unique experiences for most of the children. It is here that they may need the most help and encouragement. Also, it is important to help the children realize the importance of moving through the Stretch Steps with *quality* movement; this concept will need nurturing. While you will also want to be alert to social and safety factors as the children move through the other obstacles, those challenges are of a more general nature and can be more easily self-directed.

The obstacle course nature of these lessons provides an excellent opportunity to work with the children in developing their serial memory skills. Try to give the challenges for the first two obstacles concurrently. For example, in Lesson 1, demonstrate the first challenge listed under Beginning Stretch Steps I, and then demonstrate the first Tunnel Challenge. Then go to the circle and explain that the children should find their own way to go around the circle. Ask for ideas and demonstrate one way of moving. Throughout the lesson frequently remind the children to keep exploring new ways to go around the circle.

The Stretch Steps challenges may actually have to be demonstrated. Be specific as to whether the children should step into the spaces with one foot or both feet. Should they step over the rubber bands or on them? The children need to solve some very specific movement problems, but the problems are of a nature that allows for great success. The youngsters will be very pleased that they can move with such good control. Again, it is important to emphasize that the quality you are looking for is careful, controlled movement, not speed. The way to get to that point is to continually exclaim about the terrific movement you see!

Making and Arranging Stretch Steps

Each lesson is accompanied by a diagram of a possible room arrangement for that particular lesson. Space and equipment, however, more accurately dictate the arrangement you will use. The Stretch Steps are pleasingly economical to build. The boards are simply two-by-fours, anywhere from 6 feet to 8 feet in length. (Before deciding on the length, figure out how you will transport them and store them.) It is imperative that you carefully sand the boards so as to remove any rough edges and the possibility of splinters. As with the balance beams, it is fun to write the children's names on the beams with permanent markers.

Medium- to large-sized rubber bands can be purchased at a nominal cost. Loop five or six rubber bands together to form one rung of the steps. Simply loop the outside rubber band over the two-by-four and slide it to its correct position on the ladder. To construct the Divided Stretch Step, make a longer rubber band rope. String this rope through the center loop of each rung and tie it or loop it together at both ends.

The Limbo Rope is actually a long rubber band rope (constructed identically to the rungs of the Stretch Steps) stretched between two chairs. Be sure to anchor the rope securely and insist that the children use the rope safely: There should be no snapping or pulling of the rope. There should be no jumping over the rope.

The tunnel needed for Lesson 1 can be constructed any number of ways. Blankets can be placed over tables or chairs—or use your parachute. The good old reliable refrigerator boxes make great tunnels. Tumbling mats can also be placed across chairs.

When using a circle as a part of your obstacle course, be sure to mark a specific circle. Our favored colored spots are most versatile for this purpose. The spots can be laid out in a circular pattern, and use one single uniquely colored spot to indicate where to start moving. Gym tape can also be used to make a circle. (Make a dotted line rather than a solid line.)

LESSON 1

Aerobics (Warm-up)

Equipment: Lively music makes it more interesting.

Do any 2- or 3-minute aerobic activity mentioned elsewhere in the book. Better yet, make up your own routine! Just remember to alternate the use of the arms and legs.

Equipment for Individual Challenges: Two or more Stretch Steps; one tunnel; a circle marked on the floor; a bell to ring. Refer to the illustration showing a possible room arrangement for this lesson. The chapter introduction tells how to construct the Stretch Steps, and it offers suggestions for making a tunnel.

Specific challenges will be listed for the Stretch Steps and the Tunnel. The children should progress from the Stretch Steps through the Tunnel and around the circle, then ring the bell to finish the circuit. If two Stretch Steps are used, then the children should be divided into two groups. As the children progress to the tunnel the groups will converge. After ringing the bell, however, the children should go back to their original group.

The teacher should focus on helping the children at the Stretch Steps. While the other activities will challenge the children, the intent is to keep the youngsters actively engaged, as opposed to standing in line waiting for a turn. Give the first challenge for the tunnel at the same time you give the first challenge for the Stretch Steps. Then ask the children to find their own way to get around the circle. After naming each challenge for the Stretch Steps and the Tunnel, encourage the children to find a different way to go around the circle.

Beginning Stretch Steps (Individuals)

1. *Walk forward, putting one foot in each space.*
2. *Walk backwards.*
3. *Jump forward.*
4. *Jump backwards.*
5. *Jump sideways.*
6. *Tiptoe forward.*
7. *Tiptoe backwards.*
8. *Hop forward.*

Tunnel Challenges (Individuals)

1. *Crawl through on your hands and knees.*
2. *Go forward doing the duck walk.*

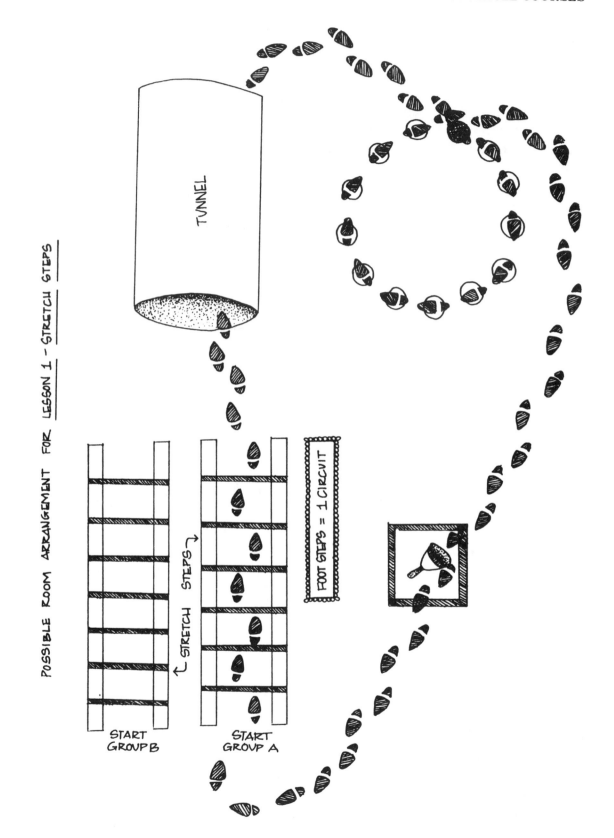

POSSIBLE ROOM ARRANGEMENT FOR LESSON 1 - STRETCH STEPS

TUNNEL

STRETCH STEPS

FOOT STEPS = 1 CIRCUIT

START GROUP B

START GROUP A

3. *Walk sideways. Will you step with your feet together, or will you cross your feet?*

4. *Lie down on your back and slide backwards. (This means that your head will lead.)*

5. *Walk through on your hands and feet. Will you go forward or backward?*

6. *Lie down on your side and wiggle, head first.*

7. *Lie on your side and move feet first.*

8. *Squat on your hands and feet; jump through the tunnel like a frog.*

Equipment for Partner Challenges: Same as for Individual Challenges.

Again, the challenges for the Stretch Steps and the Tunnel should be given concurrently. Partners will complete the obstacle course together, including the circle and the bell, making sure they stay connected in some way.

Partner Stretch Steps

All of the following challenges involve moving across the Stretch Steps while stepping inside the spaces.

1. *Partners stand one behind the other and walk forward.*

2. *Face each other and hold hands. When you get to the end of the Steps, keep hold of one another and walk back to the start; this gives the other person a chance to go backwards.*

3. *Both of you walk backwards. How will you hold onto your partner?*

4. *Jump sideways with your partner.*

5. *Face your partner and hold hands. Both of you jump. Then jump back to the start so the other person gets to go backwards.*

6. *Can you find a way to move with your partner so you are both crouched down in the medium level?*

Partner Tunneling

1. *Lie on your side facing your partner. Wiggle together head first through the tunnel.*

2. *Can you both crouch down and find a way to go through the tunnel together?*

3. *Leap Frog through the tunnel with your partner. (See Stunts and Tumbling Lesson 1.)*

4. *Face your partner and hold hands. Walk sideways while crossing and uncrossing your feet.*

5. *One of you lie down on your tummy. Let your partner* **help** *push or pull you through the tunnel. Do it again, changing jobs.*

6. *Sit back to back with your partner, with your elbows locked together. Can you push and pull yourselves through the tunnel?*

Uh-Oh! (Group)

Equipment: Stretch Steps, tunnel, circle marked on the floor; four to eight colored spots; bell or whistle for the teacher. Leave the room arranged as indicated at the beginning of the lesson.

The children move freely about the room, going across the Stretch Steps, through the Tunnel, and around the circle as they choose. When the whistle is blown the children must stop right where they are and stand still. Practice this once or twice.

Now comes the Uh-Oh part. Place one or two of the colored spots on the floor within the spaces of the Stretch Steps. This time when the whistle blows, any child who is standing on a colored spot is caught. The consequences for being caught can be something silly like standing next to the teacher while jumping up and down five times, or flapping your arms like a bird ten times. It is important not to embarrass the children, so the consequences can be performed while the other children start to move again. Any self-conscious child may choose to forego the consequences.

As the game progresses, put more and more spots down in the Stretch Steps spaces. If the children become reluctant to move across the Stretch Steps, you may call out a general direction, such as, "Everyone across the steps!"

Space Ball (Group)

Equipment: Stretch Steps; one large ball for every two children; tunnel; colored spots.

The partners stand across from one another on the opposite sides of the Stretch Steps. Each set of partners should have a Stretch Steps space in between them. The partners simply try to bounce the ball to one another, with the ball bouncing in the space each time.

If there are not enough Stretch Steps spaces for each set of partners, let other partners work at the tunnel or the circle. Encourage them to invent their own game with their partner and the ball.

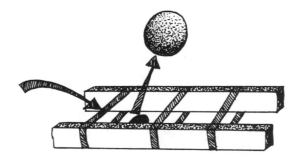

LESSON 2

Who Says? (Warm-up)

Equipment: None.

Get the children warmed up and ready to listen and move by playing a fast-paced game of Who Says? You give the children a direction, such as, "Jump up and down." Before moving, the children respond, "Who says?" The teacher picks out one child's name and answers, "Amy says!" The class then proceeds to jump until the teacher gives another direction. Before the children begin each new direction they always ask, "Who says?" With each direction the teacher uses another child's name. (To limit the number of activities and still use each child's name, the teacher may want to use two or three names for each direction given.)

Equipment for Individual Challenges: Two or more Stretch Steps; one or two tumbling mats; one or two beanbags; one or two riding toys; one or two circles marked on the floor; one or two tambourines or other noise makers; one or two bouncing balls. Refer to the illustration showing a possible room arrangement for this lesson.

Specific challenges will be listed for the Stretch Steps and the tumbling mat, but the teacher should focus on helping the children at the Stretch Steps. The children should progress from the Steps to the tumbling mat to the riding toy and finally to the tambourine. The class can be divided into two groups, and the children can stay in their own groups if there are two of each kind of equipment.

More Stretch Steps (Individuals)

1. *Move sideways by crossing and uncrossing your feet.*
2. *Move by taking very **high** steps. Will you go forward, backwards, or sideways?*
3. *Jump in the spaces, following each jump with a clap.*
4. *Do the crab walk; try to keep from stepping on the rubber bands.*
5. *Move by stepping **on** the rubber bands.*
6. *Jump **on** the rubber bands.*
7. *After stepping into each space, bounce the ball one time.*

Tumbling Mats and Beanbags (Individuals)

1. *Balance the beanbag on your hips while crawling backwards down the mat.*
2. *Jump down the mat while holding the beanbag between your knees.*
3. *Walk while **balancing** the beanbag on your foot.*

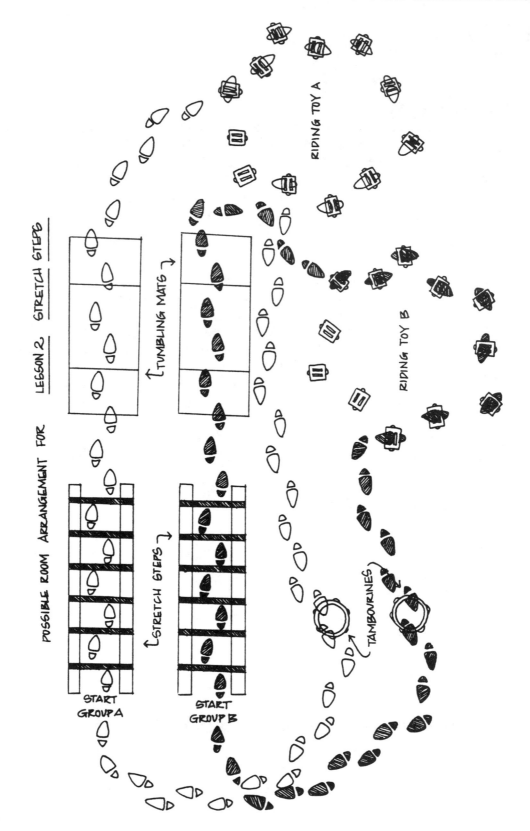

POSSIBLE ROOM ARRANGEMENT FOR LESSON 2 STRETCH STEPS

↑ TUMBLING MATS

↑ STRETCH STEPS

START GROUP A

START GROUP B

TAMBOURINES

RIDING TOY A

RIDING TOY B

4. *Do the crab walk while balancing the beanbag on your tummy. Will you go forward or backwards?*

5. *Do the Log Roll down the mat. Hold the beanbag in your hands as you go.*

6. *Walk while **balancing** the beanbag on your head.*

7. *Invent your own way to move. Will you hold the beanbag or balance it?*

Equipment for Partner Challenges   Same as for Individual Challenges.

Remember, the challenges for the Stretch Steps and the Tumbling Mats should be given concurrently. Partners will complete the Stretch Steps and the Tumbling Mats together, but they will need to move individually on the riding toys. They could meet again to shake the tambourine together.

More Partner Stretch Steps

1. *Hold hands and walk side by side while crossing and uncrossing feet.*

2. *Move in the spaces with one partner crouched down in the medium level and the other person up high. Don't forget to stay connected.*

3. *Walk one behind the other with your feet on the **boards**.*

4. *Face each other and hold hands. Move down the Steps together stepping **on** the rubber bands.*

5. *Each partner stands on one of the boards, and the two partners face each other and hold hands. Walk sideways together on the boards.*

6. *Follow your partner. You do not need to be connected. Jump on a rubber band, then in a space, then on a rubber band, then in a space, and so on.*

Partner Mat Challenges

Some of these activities will require a beanbag.

1. *Stand side by side with your partner and hold hands. Hop down the mat.*

2. *You and your partner hold a beanbag between your hips. Move down the mat.*

3. *Find a way to move down the mat with one of you being up high and the other being down low. Stay connected.*

4. *Get on your knees one behind the other. The back person holds the ankles of the front person. Now both of you crawl forward. Then trade positions and try again.*

5. *Find another way to hold the beanbag between you and your partner while moving down the mat.*

6. *Stand back to back with your partner with your elbows locked. Walk down the mat. Then trade positions and try again.*

Human Cave (Group)

Equipment: One or two sets of Stretch Steps.

The children need partners. The children line up side by side on the boards, standing across from their partners. Everyone reaches up high above their head and holds their partner's hands. The front couple lets go of hands and one stands behind the other at the entrance to the "cave." They walk through the cave, carefully stepping in the spaces. When the couple reaches the end of the cave, they again step up on the boards and hold hands. Everyone on the boards slides one space towards the front. The next front couple then proceeds through the cave. Continue until everyone gets a turn to go through the cave.

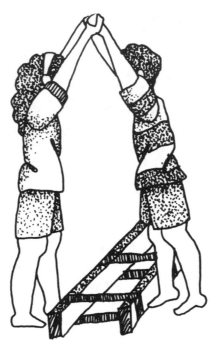

Double Stretch Steps (Group)

Equipment: Two sets of Stretch Steps; one tumbling mat.

Stack the two sets of Stretch Steps on top of each other. Use a tumbling mat under the Stretch Steps. Make sure the top rubber bands are lined up with those underneath them. The top set of rubber bands will now be 4 inches off the floor. This can be quite a challenge for the children.

Give the children some simple challenges to start with as they adapt to the extra height of the rubber bands. Caution them to take their time and to pick up their feet! If you need ideas, use any of the challenges from Beginning Stretch Steps in Lesson 1 or More Stretch Steps in Lesson 2.

LESSON 3

Dance, Dance, Dance! (Warm-up)

Equipment: Dance music. Why not try something unusual, such as Calypso music? Or pick your own favorite—rock'n'roll, twist, or bunny hop?

Encourage the children to dance alone or with a friend. What a great way to loosen up and get moving!

Equipment for Individual Challenges: Two or more Divided Stretch Steps; one or two tumbling mats; one or two rubber band ropes; two or four chairs; three or six beanbags; one or two targets (hula hoops, boxes, or spots). Refer to the illustration showing a possible room arrangement for this lesson. This chapter's introduction tells how to construct the Divided Stretch Steps, and it offers suggestions for using the rubber band rope.

Specific challenges will be listed for the Divided Stretch Steps and the Limbo Rope. There will be no specific challenges for the tumbling mats, but encourage the children to find different ways to get from one end of the mat to the other. Remind them to move safely and to take turns. At the beanbag toss, each person may take three tosses. Encourage the children to find different ways to toss the beanbags or to move farther away from the target.

Divide the children into groups according to the amount of equipment available. If there is sufficient equipment, the children may be able to stay in their individual groups throughout the circuit. The children should progress from the Stretch Steps to the Limbo Rope to the tumbling mat to the beanbag toss. The teacher should give the first challenges for both the Divided Steps and the Limbo Rope at the same time.

Divided Stretch Steps (Individuals)

1. *Walk forward with one foot in each space.*
2. *Walk backwards with one foot in each space.*
3. *Walk forward on your hands and feet.*
4. (Put colored spots under alternate spaces.) *Walk forward stepping only on the spots. Now jump forward landing only on the spots.*
5. Lay the spots under the spaces as shown in the diagram. *When two spots are side by side, jump. When one spot is alone, hop.*
6. *Jump sideways, then forward, then sideways, then forward.*
7. *Walk down just one side of the Divided Steps.*
8. *Walk backward down one side of the Divided Steps.*

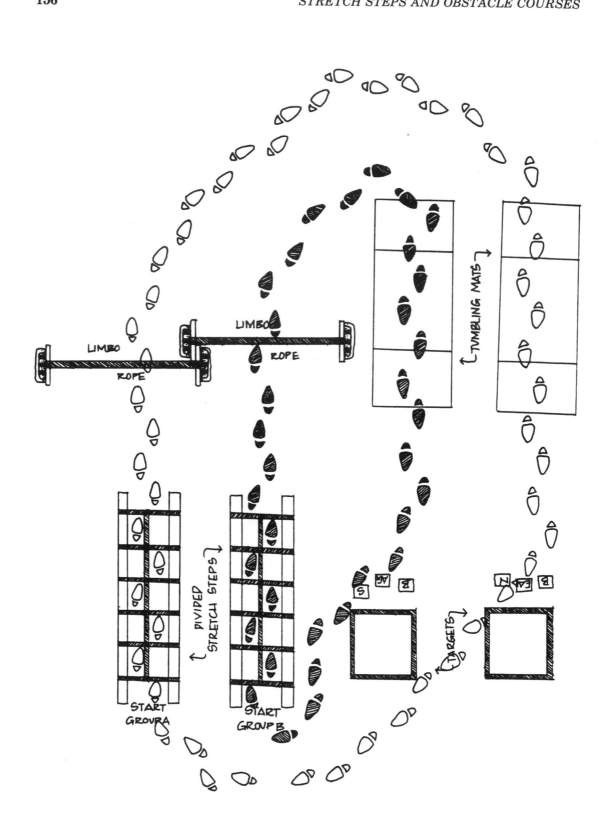

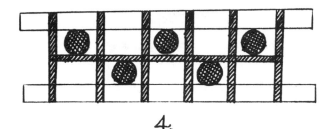

4.

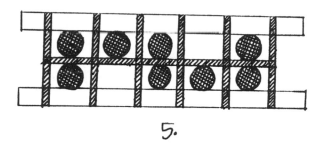

5.

9. *Stand in place, with one foot in each space. Jump in place, crossing and uncrossing your feet.*

Limbo Rope (Individuals)

Caution the children about using the rope safely. *Do not pull on the rope or snap it.*

1. *Go under the rope without touching it.*
2. *Slide on your back, head first.*
3. *Slide on your back, feet first.*
4. *Slide under on your stomach, head first.*
5. *Slide under on your stomach, feet first.*
6. *Lie on your side and go under, head first.*
7. *Lie on your side and go under, feet first.*
8. *Do a log roll under the rope.*
9. *Do the seal walk under the rope. (See Seal Balance, p. 129).*
10. *Do the crab walk under the rope. Will you go forward or backward?*

Equipment for Partner Challenges: Same as for Individual Challenges.

Again, the challenges for the Stretch Steps and the Limbo Rope should be given concurrently. Partners will work together for the steps and the rope, but they may work individually on the mat and the beanbag target.

Divided Stretch Steps With a Partner

1. *Walk one behind the other, with one foot in each space.*
2. *Face each other and hold hands. Walk with one foot in each space.*
3. *(Place one color of spots under alternate spaces as in Step 4 of Divided Stretch Steps. Place another color of spots in the opposite spaces.) One of you walks on one color of spots, and your partner walks on the other color at the same time.*
4. *One of you jumps on one color, and your partner jumps on the other color.*

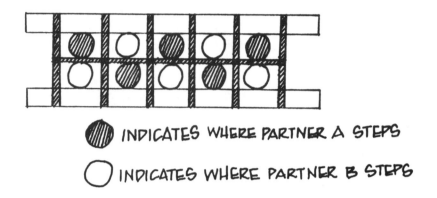

INDICATES WHERE PARTNER A STEPS

INDICATES WHERE PARTNER B STEPS

5. *Walk side by side with your partner. Each person walks on one side of the Divided Steps.*
6. *Walk side by side with your partner, each person going backwards down one side of the Divided Steps.*
7. *Face your partner and hold hands. Jump sideways down the Divided Steps.*

Limbo Rope With a Partner

1. *Lie down on your stomachs, one behind the other. The back person holds the feet of the front person and both of you wiggle under the rope.*
2. *Sit back-to-back with your partner, with your elbows locked. Slide sideways under the rope.*
3. *Lie on your side, back to back with your partner. Slide under the rope going head first.*
4. *Hold hands with your partner. Crouch down and do the duck walk under the rope.*
5. *Hold your partner's hand and do the duck walk backwards under the rope.*
6. *Lie on your back beside your partner. Hold hands and slide head first under the rope.*
7. *You and your partner invent your own way to go under the rope.*

Group Stretch (Group)

Equipment: One very long rubber band rope; two different colors of spot markers—enough for each child and the teacher to have one spot.

Lay the spot markers on the floor in a circle, alternating the colors. Each child stands in one spot. Pass a rubber band rope around the circle so each child is holding one section of the rope. The teacher should hold both ends of the rope. Instruct the children on how to best hold the rope. It is more secure if they put their hand through the two parts of the rubber band and then make a fist. The group can perform the following activities together.

1. *Walk backwards a few steps and stretch the rope.*
2. *Hold the rope up high.*
3. *Hold the rope down low.*
4. *Sit down with your legs out straight. Lean back and stretch the rope. Lean forward and relax. Repeat several times.*
5. *Stand up. Hold the rope in front of you while you jump and alternately kick each leg out in front.*
6. *Shake the rope. Shake it high and low.*
7. *Hold the rope in front of you. Pull your arms to the left and right alternately.*
8. *Children on a yellow spot take two steps back; those on an orange spot take two steps in.* Reverse.
9. *Those on a yellow spot hold the rope high; those on an orange spot hold the rope low.* Reverse.

SECTION X

Flying Disks

INTRODUCTION

The idea of a flying disk generally conjures up the picture of a hard plastic flying disk, like *the* Frisbee™. However, athletic equipment catalogues now carry an interesting variety of soft foam disks. It is these soft foam disks which are most advisable for use with preschoolers (or with any large group all hurtling disks simultaneously).

The author has never discovered the soft foam disks for sale in any retail sporting goods, department, or discount stores. The retail outlets seem to carry only the hard plastic disks. But the soft foam disks (they are generally indexed by that name) are readily available in athletic or physical education equipment catalogues.

In fact, one of the author's often used equipment sources has no fewer than six different index listings for foam disks. Let's talk a little about the variety of foam disks available. The disks can be found in either an uncoated or a vinyl-coated variety. The uncoated disks will be less expensive, and the author, on that basis, recommends the uncoated variety. The vinyl coating on the disks does not seem to add to its durability. (Any child who absolutely feels the need to take a bite out of the disk will do so even if it is vinyl coated.)

There are disks that have a more traditional shape, that is, they have rounded edges. A more economical foam disk is available that has a straight edge. There is additionally a straight-edged disk made of a harder foam material with colored tape around the edge of the disk. This particular disk is undesirable for two reasons: the foam is too hard to be comfortable and safe, and the tape is not durable. The other major problem with the straight-edged disk is that it tends to be thicker, and therefore more difficult for preschool-sized hands to manipulate. The author recommends spending a few extra dollars to purchase the round-edged disks.

Depending on your budget, you can purchase the foam disks in one color or a variety of colors. Of course, the colors will always add another dimension to your teaching. To add even more learning opportunities, there are foam disks that are imprinted with numbers, colors, shapes, and letters of the alphabet. For the totally unrestricted budget (or for a different kind of fund-raiser) it is possible to purchase flying disks imprinted with your organization's own logo.

The one constant that can be found with the disks is their diameter, which is 8 inches to 9½ inches. (Here is an opportunity for someone to invent a mini-disk or a maxi-disk.) The foam disks fly very well. The other advantage of the foam disks, other than their safety, is that they fly more slowly. That makes them more suitable for the slower reaction time of the preschoolers.

Pay close attention when looking at the equipment list for each flying disk activity. If a soft disk is listed, then the safety factor necessitates a foam disk. However, if the equipment list only indicates "flying disk," then the traditional hard plastic disk will suffice.

For some activities, "substitute" disks may be used. Paper plates (or two paper plates taped together) can be used. In other instances plastic coffee can lids are useful. (It may be just my imagination, but it seems to this author that the lids from decaffeinated coffee cans do not fly as far or as fast as those from the caffeinated coffee!) Another possible substitute is the lid from the 5-quart pails of ice cream. (There are those among us who feel compelled to sacrifice our cholesterol for the good of the preschool program.)

Transport and store the disks in an old pillowcase that has a drawstring woven through the hem of the open end. If needed, the whole sack of disks can be washed on the gentle cycle of your washing machine and line dried.

It is always a good idea to work with the children on the proper use and care of the equipment. The flying disk, with proper care and storage, can be a wonderfully fun and long-lived part of your movement program.

LESSON 1

Spin and Toss (Equipment Activity)

Equipment: One soft disk per child.

Show the children how to hold the disk by its edge (perpendicular to the floor). Ask the children if they can toss the disk straight up into the air. *Can you catch the disk without having to move very far away from your space?*

Diskacize (Warm-up)

Equipment: One flying disk per child; upbeat music ("Leroy Brown"); tape player or record player.

1. *Hold the disk with two hands above your head and do a jumping jack jump.*

2. *Hold the disk in one hand and shake it like a tambourine. Repeat with your other hand.*

3. *Move the disk around your waist by exchanging the disk from one hand to the other behind your back.*

4. *Hold the disk in two hands straight out in front of you. Kick one leg up high to kick the disk (keep hold of the disk!). Now kick with the other leg. Alternate for several kicks.*

5. *Stand in a wide stride. Hold the disk with two hands in front of your chest. Push the disk straight out; pull it back into your chest. Alternately push and pull for several counts.*

6. *Lie down on the floor using the disk as a pillow. Raise your legs up off the floor and bicycle.*

7. *Hold the disk in one hand and make big arm circles. Repeat with the other arm.*

8. *To end the song ("Leroy Brown" or another), shake the disk like a tambourine.*

Toss and Run (Individuals)

Equipment: One soft disk per child.

Show the children how to hold the disk with their thumb on top and their fingers on the bottom of the disk. Demonstrate the backhand throwing motion, with particular emphasis on the wrist action. The children will not have much accuracy at this point. Just let them each toss their own disk, then run to pick up their own disk and toss again. Before the children begin, talk with them about watching for each other when they are running! Remind the children to try tossing the disk with their other hand too.

Wheels, Wheels, Everywhere (Individuals)

Equipment: One flying disk per child.

Ask the children to name some objects that are shaped like a flying disk. One of the objects they name will most likely be a wheel or a tire. Ask the children if they can roll their "wheels" about the room. Remind them that they will be bending over, so it will take extra care to watch for each other.

1. *Use your other hand to roll the wheel.*
2. *Can you roll the wheel through your legs?*
3. *Can you roll the wheel forward away from you?*
4. *Can you roll the wheel backwards through your legs?*
5. *Can you roll the wheel sideways away from you?*

Partner Flyers (Partners)

Equipment: One soft disk for every two children.

Let the children start by just playing catch with each other. Some children will need to be encouraged to move farther away from each other, while others will need to be encouraged to get closer together.

Ask the children to find new ways to get the disk to their partner.

1. Some children will roll the disk.
2. Some children may try to kick the disk.
3. Throwing the disk backwards through the legs (like hiking a football), is popular.
4. *Try tossing the disk behind your back or under one leg.*
5. *Hold the disk by its edge and toss it backwards over your head.*
6. *Hold the disk up with one hand. Now try to bat the disk with your other hand.*

Cap Race (Groups)

Equipment: Four to six flying disks for each group; two space markers for each group.

Divide the class into groups of equal numbers. Each group should have four to six disks. Each group lines up one behind the other behind a space marker which is on the floor in front of them. Each group's other space marker should be straight across the room, 10 feet to 15 feet away.

The first person in each group will stack all her team's disks on top of her head. On the signal to run, she will run to the other end of the room while holding all of the disks on her head. When she gets to her space marker at the other end of the room, she will turn around and run back to her team.

The first person will then place all of the "caps" on top of the next player's head. The second player will then repeat the route. Continue the game until every person has had a turn to run with the "caps."

After playing the game, talk with the children about cooperating with their teammates. *If you just finished running with the caps, how could you make it easier for the next runner to get started? Would it help if you carefully place the caps on top of the next runner's head?*

After the children become familiar with the game, add some further challenges. For example, require the children to run backwards when coming back across the room to their team.

LESSON 2

Flat Hat (Equipment Activity)

Equipment: One soft disk per child.

Ask the children if they can wear the disk like a hat while they move about the room.

1. *Will the hat stay on your head if you move sideways or backwards?*
2. *Can you stoop down to touch the floor and still balance the hat on your head? (Can you do it without holding the hat with your hand?)*
3. *Will you move fast or slowly if you want the hat to stay on your head?*

Footloose (Warm-up)

Equipment: One flying disk per child; tape or record of the song "Footloose" (or other upbeat music); tape player or record player.

1. *Lay the disk on the floor and stand beside it. Jump sideways over the disk; then jump back the other direction. Repeat the jumps several times.* (Continuous jumps will be more of a challenge, and some students will be able to do that.)
2. *Hold your disk in two hands. Push the disk straight up above your head to the left; bring it down to your chest; push it straight up to the right; down to your chest, and so on.*
3. *Lay the disk on the floor and stand behind it. Jump forward over the disk. Then jump backward over the disk. Continue the jumps for several turns.* (Some children will find it difficult to jump backwards. Let them turn around to jump.)
4. *Hold the disk with two hands high over your head. Run in a small circle to the right; reverse directions and run in a small circle to the left.*
5. *Hold the disk in one hand in front of you. Tap the disk with your other hand eight times. Hold the disk behind your back and tap it eight times with your other hand. Repeat the front and back sequence.*
6. *Hold the disk against your tummy while jumping. Try to do a twist jump, twisting your hips to the left and right as you jump.*

Floating Disks (Individuals)

Equipment: One soft disk per child.

Talk with the children again about what it means to balance a disk on your head or your hand: *That's right, it means that the disk will stay there by itself, without being held. We've already tried balancing the disks on our heads. If you* balance the disk on the back of your hand and gently wave your hand, it looks like the disk is floating. Where else can you balance the disk and make it float? As the children explore, point out all of the wonderful ideas you are seeing.

Do you always have to stay standing up as you balance the disk? Where can you balance the disk if you are lying on your back? If you are on your hands and knees where can you balance the disk? Can you still make it float by gently waving your body?

Flexible Folding Flyer Feet (Partners)

Equipment: One flying disk for every two children; one carpet sample for each child (or tumbling mats or a carpeted floor).

Partners start sitting back to back. Then they need to slide far enough away from each other so each of them can lie on their back. The partners need to lie on their backs (on their carpet squares), head to head, but without their heads touching.

One of the partners holds the disk between her feet. She then rolls backwards and passes the disk to her partner's legs. Her partner will have also rolled backwards and will have his feet up in the air waiting to receive the disk.

Patty-Cake Disk (Partners)

Equipment: One flying disk per child.

Each child should have her own disk. Partners will face each other while holding the disk in one hand. Teach the children the following rhyme:

Patty cake, patty cake,
Disk is fine;
I can hold the disk
With these knees of mine.

As the children repeat the first two lines above, they will clap their partner's two hands. Each person will clap her own hands as she says the third line. On the fourth line of the poem, each child should hold the disk with the body part named. For example, in the rhyme above, the children should put the disk between their own knees.

The disk should be held with the knees while the rhyme is repeated. Each time the rhyme is repeated, a new body part will be named.

To further challenge the children, let them try the game using only one disk for two children. Thus, when they hold the disk, both children will be holding the same disk with their knees.

Pizza Delivery (Group)

Equipment: One flying disk.

The children will sit in a circle to play this game. Ask the children to name their favorite kind of pizza. Then announce that you are going to play a game called "Pizza Delivery." Ask the children if they can guess what you will use for the pizza. *That's right, the disk will be the pizza.*

You, the teacher, will demonstrate the game. As you walk around the outside of the circle, carrying the pizza, explain that you are the pizza delivery person. When the pizza delivery person lays the pizza on the floor behind someone's back, the delivery person says "ding dong," as if the doorbell is ringing. After you say "ding dong," the entire group will yell "pizza delivery."

The person to whom you delivered the pizza must jump up and chase you around the circle back to his own space. Leave the pizza laying on the floor: it makes a good marker so the runner knows where to stop. Then it is the chaser's turn to be the pizza delivery person. However, if the pizza delivery person is caught by the chaser, she must sit in the middle of the circle for one turn. (It is less intimidating if the middle becomes the "kitchen," where the person who was caught must take one turn making a pizza. You could even equip the "kitchen" with a rolling pin and pizza pan.

LESSON 3

Hold It! (Equipment Activity)

Equipment: One soft disk per child.

Challenge the children to find different ways to hold the disk. For example, they can hold the disk between their elbows, their knees, the back of their knees, and so on. The disks can also be held in the following ways:

1. Between the forearm and upper arm.
2. Under the arm.
3. Between the chin and chest.
4. Between the wrist and leg.
5. Between the foot and forehead.

Disk-Go-Round (Warm-up)

Equipment: One flying disk per child.

1. *Hold the disk in one hand. Move that hand behind your back and put the disk in your other hand. As quickly as you can, move the disk around your waist, exchanging it from one hand to the other behind your back. Move the disk in the other direction, too.*
2. *Move the disk around your ankles.*
3. *Make the disk go around your knees.*
4. *Make the disk go around just one leg.*
5. *With your legs wide apart, put the disk through your legs; grab it from behind your legs using your other hand. Bring the disk around to the front and repeat the motion.*

Jumping Disks (Individuals)

Equipment: One flying disk per child.

Hold the disk vertically between your feet. While still holding the disk, jump into the air and grab the disk with your hand. The second time you jump, try to grab the disk with your other hand.

Disk Bump (Individuals)

Equipment: One flying disk per child.

Start on the floor on your hands and knees. Place the disk on your bottom. Give a little jump with your feet, keeping your arms straight and strong. This should make the disk fly forward and land on the floor in front of you. Remember to land on your **feet**, *not your knees. And keep your arms strong so you don't land on your nose!*

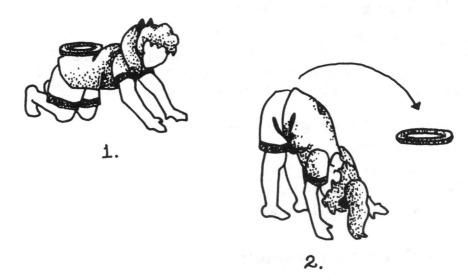

Tricky Tosses (Individuals)

Equipment: One soft disk per child.

Let the children warm up by tossing the disk straight up in the air and catching it. Ask the children if they can toss the disk and then do a trick before catching it.

1. *Toss the disk; clap your hands; catch the disk.*
2. *Toss the disk; clap your knees* (or tummy, or sides, or bottom); *catch the disk.*
3. *Toss the disk; turn around before catching the disk.*

Musical Disks (Partners)

Equipment: One flying disk for every two children; music source.

Divide the class into pairs. The partners should lay the disk on the floor in front of them. When the music is playing, the partners move together about the room. When the music stops, the partners quickly move to the nearest disk, pick it up, and find a way to hold the disk between them.

Before starting the music each time, suggest different ways for the children to move. Or, encourage the partners to find their own new ways each time the music starts.

Remind the children that they don't always have to stay standing in order to hold the disk—or to move about the room!

Tire Targets (Partners)

Equipment: One soft disk for every two children; one bicycle tire (or hula hoop) for every two children.

Divide the class into pairs. Each set of partners will need one bicycle tire and one soft disk. Help the children to decide who will be the first person to be the tire "holder," and who will be the first to be the disk "tosser."

Talk about different ways to hold the tire away from your body so you won't be hit by the flying disk. *Be sure to leave room for the disk to go through the tire. The tire can be held next to your side or above your head.*

The tosser should move about the room, tossing his disk into each tire in turn. You may challenge the tossers to move closer to or farther away from the tire targets. When you give the signal to change, the tosser will trade jobs with his original partner. His partner should have an equal amount of time to be the tosser.

For each tosser's second turn, have the tire holder find a way to gently move the tire. There are several ways to do this:

1. *Swing the tire back and forth beside you.*
2. *Swing the tire back and forth above your head.*
3. *Roll the tire back and forth on the floor.*
4. *Slowly spin the tire about its axis.*

While the tire is *slowly* moving, the tosser should again move about the room, trying to toss the disk through each tire.

"Caps for Sale" (Group)

Equipment: One soft disk per child; a copy of the book *Caps for Sale.* (Esphyr Slobodkina, Harper and Row, 1968); preschool climber (or several chairs or other space markers).

The majority of preschoolers will be familiar with the story "Caps for Sale," but to make sure everyone knows the story, read it to the class before starting this activity. After reading the story, tell the children that you will be acting out the story. *The teacher will be the peddler. The climber will be the tree. Who will the children be? That's right, the children will be the monkeys.*

You will gather all of the disk "caps" and walk about the room wearing them on your head while saying, *"Caps for sale. Who will buy my caps? Fifty cents a cap. Caps for sale."* Just as in the story, the peddler will become tired and sit down to rest. She will lay the caps on the floor beside her. The monkeys then go pick up the caps—one cap for each monkey. The monkeys carry their caps with them and go to the "tree."

The peddler (you) awakes to find the caps missing and goes in search of the caps. Once you "find" the monkeys with the caps, go through the motions of scolding and begging for the caps. The monkeys will mimic your actions. After you entice the monkeys to throw down their caps, the children no doubt will want to play the game again. (And after you stand beneath the tree while the monkeys throw down their caps, you will understand the necessity for soft disks.)

Rhythm and Dance

INTRODUCTION

A variety set of rhythm instruments, for up to twenty-five players, can be purchased quite reasonably through various preschool/elementary equipment catalogues. The instrument sets might include rhythm sticks, tone blocks with mallets, sand blocks, wrist bells, triangles with strikers, cymbals, maracas, drums with mallets, tambourines, and jingle taps. The wide selection of instruments, and the fact that twenty-five children can be accommodated, makes these rhythm sets seem like a terrific bargain. Such a set would provide a real boost to your rhythms unit.

But don't let budget constraints stop you from teaching rhythm and dance activities. In fact, if you have been collecting the equipment listed up to this point in the book, you already have a rhythm instrument for each child. The 5-quart plastic ice cream buckets make excellent drums. The children can use their hands to beat the drums. Mallets can be made very reasonably. Cut 8-inch to 10-inch lengths of ⅝-inch or ¾-inch dowel rod. Cut a small piece of durable fabric to be the mallet head, and stuff this fabric with recycled nylon hose or other fabric. Secure the mallet head to the dowel with a rubber band. The mallet heads could even be color-coded, and that opens up a whole other realm of movement possibilities. Or you might just be able to start with only half enough mallets, leaving the other half of the children to use their hands to beat the drums. And now you have a terrific learning-to-share experience!

Use the lids from the 5-quart ice cream buckets to make tambourines. Use an electric drill with a very small bit to drill three holes at even spaces around the edge of the lid. Secure one jingle bell at each of those spots by threading a twist-tie through the hole and the bell and twisting until the bell is secure. If the lids are stacked carefully on top of each other several lids can be drilled at the same time.

Wood blocks and sand blocks are also extremely easy to make. Don't hesitate to scour your community for donations of scrap lumber. Half-inch or ⅝-inch pine or other soft wood is the easiest to work with. Simply cut the wood into the desired sizes (anywhere from 3 inches by 5 inches to 4 inches by 6 inches) and sand the edges smooth. Use self-affixing knobs or screw the knobs on from the bottom side. Sand blocks can be made by tacking or stapling coarse-grade sandpaper onto the blocks.

Rhythm sticks can be made simply cutting lengths of dowel rod to the desired length. Remove the sharp and rough edges with a sander. Dowel rod that is $\frac{5}{16}$ inches up to $\frac{5}{8}$ inches in diameter would work best. Rhythm sticks that are anywhere from 8 inches to 10 inches in length are most appropriate for preschoolers.

Both the rhythm sticks and the sand blocks can be painted if so desired. These two woodworking projects would be excellent projects for school-related industrial arts classes, 4-H clubs, or other youth groups looking for service projects. And don't forget about your senior citizen organizations. You will find any number of skills waiting to be tapped!

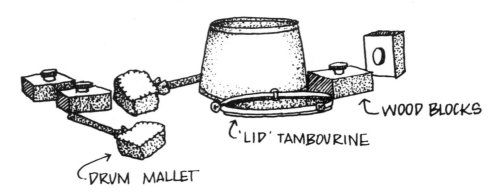
DRUM MALLET · 'LID' TAMBOURINE · WOOD BLOCKS

LESSON 1

Tambourines Everywhere (Warm-up)

Equipment: One tambourine per child.

The children are in a scattered formation. *Hold the tambourine in one hand and shake it everywhere. Shake it up high, down low, around your waist, through your legs, out to the side, and behind your back! Now put the tambourine in your other hand and try it again. Where can you shake your tambourine?*

I Can Tap My . . . (Individuals)

Equipment: One tambourine per child.

The children are in a scattered formation. Call out a body part for the children to tap with their tambourine. Then let them call out body parts to tap. Remember to frequently change hands. Keep going until you have exhausted all possibilities.

Isolated Shakes (Individuals)

Equipment: The teacher needs one "real" tambourine.

The children are in a scattered formation, with lots of room between each other. When you shake the tambourine, the children are to shake just one body part as you call it out. For example, if the children are to use an arm, they explore shaking that one arm everywhere, all around their body.

Try having them shake some body parts while standing, others while sitting, and still others while lying down. Let the children explore shaking one leg while standing and then while lying down. Encourage the children to concentrate on shaking just the parts named and not to randomly shake their whole body. But it is fun to end the activity by "shaking everything."

Four- and five-year-olds can be challenged to shake two different body parts at one time, for example, one arm and one leg, or just the right arm and right leg, and so on. But the shaking will have to be at a slower, gentler pace so the children can maintain control.

Tambourine Mime (Partners)

Equipment: One tambourine per child.

Assign partners. Decide which partner is taller and which is shorter. The shorter partner gets to be the first leader. The partners stand facing one another. The leader shakes his tambourine up high, down low, to the side, and so forth. His partner tries to follow his actions. Emphasize to the leaders that they should try to move so their partners can follow their actions. Move slowly so your partner can copy your movements. Frequently change leaders.

This activity can also be done with the partners moving about the room. The follower would then want to be behind the leader. The leader, then, not only gets to choose how to shake the tambourine, but also how to move about the room. Encourage the children to focus on both of those activities.

Tambourine Exchange (Group)

Equipment: One tambourine per child; the teacher should have a "real" tambourine.

Each child has her own tambourine, and you start with a "real" tambourine. Ask the children to move in a certain manner and/or a specific direction while shaking their tambourines. When you strike your tambourine loudly two times, everyone stops moving and exchanges tambourines with another person. This continues until each person has had a turn to use the "real" tambourine.

Some examples of the many possible movement challenges are:

1. *Move forward and tap your knees.*
2. *Gallop and tap your hip.*
3. *Tiptoe backwards and tap your wrist.*
4. *Take giant steps backwards and tap your tummy.*
5. *Move sideways and tap your head.*

Hokey Pokey Tambourines (Group)

Equipment: One tambourine per child; tape or record of "The Hokey Pokey" is optional.

The children form a circle. As "The Hokey Pokey" is played, or as they sing it, the children tap that body part with their tambourine. For example:

"Put your right hand in,"—*Put a hand in the circle and tap that hand with the tambourine.*

"Put your right hand out,"—*Put that same hand outside the circle and tap with the tambourine.*

"Put your right hand in and shake it all about."—*Put same hand in circle and tap it with the tambourine.*

"You do the Hokey Pokey and turn yourself around,"—*Turn in a small circle and tap tambourine with your hand.*

"That's what it's all about!"—*Raise tambourine over head and shake it.*

Trembling Teacher (Group)

Equipment: One tambourine for the teacher; tumbling mat recommended.

This is not an activity for a faint-hearted teacher (or probably for one who wears glasses)! If there is another adult in the room it is helpful to let that adult shake the tambourine. The teacher lies down on the tumbling mat with the children circled around her. The teachers shows the children how her leg starts shaking when she hears the tambourine, and the problem is she can't get her leg to stop shaking. Invite the children to help you get your leg stopped. They will gladly do so.

But after that leg is stopped, oops, the other leg starts shaking. And when that leg is stopped, an arm starts shaking, and so on. (The tambourine is being played this whole time.) After the children get the teacher's movements completely stopped, instruct them to sit in a circle around you again. Tell them you are going to move on to another activity. But alas, when the children are settled, look out—the teacher's leg starts shaking again! Oh no, here we go again!

LESSON 2

Drums Everywhere (Warm-up)

Equipment: One drum per child.

The children are in a scattered formation. Let the children experiment with beating the drum.

1. *Do you always have to beat the drum hard, or can you also strike it softly?*
2. *Can you beat the drum slowly and then very, very fast?*
3. *Beat the drum while you hold it high, low, around your waist, through your legs, out to the side, and even behind your back!*
4. *Now try it again with the drum in your other hand.*
5. *Where else can you hold the drum and strike it? Can you hold the drum between your knees? Under an arm?*
6. The plastic ice cream bucket drums can even be worn on their heads while they play them, but warn them to play softly.

Move Strongly, Move Lightly (Individuals)

Equipment: One drum and one triangle for the teacher.

As the teacher beats the drum strongly, the children move the way the drum makes them feel. *How does the drum make you feel?* (Elicit the words "hard" or "strong.") Keep using a strong beat, but challenge the children to move in various directions and with various types of movement. Be sure to use an uneven beat when asking the children to move with a gallop or a slide.

Introduce the triangle. It's easy for the children to guess the name of the instrument because it has the same name as its shape. *Move the way the triangle makes you feel like moving. If the drum is "hard," then the triangle is . . .* ("soft"). *If the drum is "strong," then the triangle is . . .* ("light"). Again, vary the directions and types of movement. Then alternate between the drum and the triangle so the children must choose an appropriate movement response.

Good Vibrations (Individuals)

Equipment: One or more triangles.

Show the children how to play the triangle. Demonstrate how the triangle makes a different sound if it is held by a string while it is played, rather than held by the triangle itself. Give each child a turn to strike the triangle both by holding the string and then by holding the triangle itself.

Give each child the opportunity to feel the vibration (buzz or tingle) of the triangle when it is struck. Stop in front of each child and strike the triangle; instruct the child to grab hold of the triangle as soon as it is struck. (If the vibration continues up the string into your own hand, you will know that the child felt it also.) Explain that it is this vibration that helps the triangle make its sound.

Reach and Recoil (Individuals)

Equipment: One drum and one triangle for the teacher.
The children are in a scattered formation.

1. Beat the drum strongly and show the children how to reach out strongly with one arm. *Pull the arm back* (recoil) *strongly on the next beat. Moving with the beat, keep reaching and recoiling with that arm. Take your arm high, low, around your waist, through your legs, out to the side, and so on. Then try the other arm.*

2. *Next try one leg while standing; give the other leg a turn. Try both legs while lying down.*

3. Reach and recoil with the triangle. *Will the movements be hard or soft, strong or light?* The movements should be gentle and slow, and as the sound reverberates, the movement may be continuous. The children move their arms and legs, as they did with the drum.

4. *Can we only reach with our arms or legs? What else can we use for reaching?* Let the children name body parts to reach with, and try each one. Do some movements strongly and some lightly. (But the children really do prefer the strong movement!) *Don't be bashful. Remember, you can reach with your elbows, shoulders, knees, hips, bottoms, tummy, head, and even your tongue. Reach and recoil with all of the parts of your body at once.* Make sure the children have plenty of space before starting.

REACH!

RECOIL!

Loud or Soft (Partners)

Equipment: One drum for every two children.

Assign partners and decide which one will move first and which will sit first. If the ice cream bucket drums are being used the sitter can actually turn the drum upside down and sit on it. Or the sitter may choose to play the drum along with the teacher.

Does the drum always have to be played loudly? Can it also be played softly? If the drum is played loudly, the mover should move strongly about the room. If the drum is played softly she should move lightly. Frequently change the beat, also, and encourage the children to move with the beat: slowly, fast, galloping, and so forth. Stop frequently to allow the partners to trade places.

Circle Drums (Group)

Equipment: One drum per child, or a combination of drums and tambourines.

The children form a circle facing counterclockwise, each child holding his drum. Practice with the children so they can beat the drum four times, with a slight pause after the four beats. This dance will all be done to the count of four.

1. *Hold the drum high four beats, and march forward.*
2. *Hold the drum low four beats, and march forward.*
3. *Hold the drum in front of your tummy four beats, and march forward.*
4. *Hold the drum behind your back four beats, and march forward.*
5. Reverse the direction of the circle and repeat steps 1 through 4.
6. *Four beats and march four steps into the center of the circle.*
7. *Four beats and march four steps back out of the circle.*

Before repeating the dance give the children the choice of using a drum or a tambourine.

LESSON 3

How Do You Feel? (Warm-up)

Equipment: One each of the following instruments for the teacher: tambourine, drum, triangle, maracas, and rhythm sticks or wood blocks.

Play the instruments one at a time and encourage the children to move the way the instrument makes them feel like moving. Frequently change the beat: even or uneven, fast or slow. Challenge the children to sometimes move at different levels and in various directions.

Listen and Remember (Individuals)

Equipment: One each of the following instruments: tambourine, drum, triangle, maracas, and rhythm sticks or wood blocks.

As you introduce each instrument, name the movement that goes with the instrument. For example, *when you hear the drum you should march.* Practice the marching for a bit. Then introduce *the tambourine, which means you should gallop.* (Be sure to use an uneven rhythm.) Practice galloping to the tambourine for a bit. Then alternate the use of the drum and the tambourine, challenging the children to remember how to move to each sound.

Add still another instrument, such as the triangle, which might mean tiptoe. Be sure to practice that instrument alone for a bit before mixing in the other instruments. The age and ability level of your group will determine the number of variations they can remember. Don't be afraid to challenge them. They might even remember better than you do!

Copy the Beat (Individuals)

Equipment: Give each child one instrument from the variety of instruments you have available: tambourines, drums, triangles, maracas or rhythm sticks, one drum for the teacher.

Play a beat on your drum. The children use their instruments to try to copy the beat. After several turns let the children *quickly* change instruments with a classmate. (The children will move quickly if the teacher only gives them until the count of five and then immediately starts a new beat.) Be creative. Vary not only the beat, but also the manner in which you play the instrument, for example, up high, down low, to the side. If possible, continue the activity until each child gets a turn to play each instrument.

Buddy Band *(Partners)*

Equipment: One instrument for each child; use a variety of instruments.

The children choose a partner who has a *different* instrument than their own. The partners move together about the room while playing their instruments.

1. *Do you always have to move forward?*
2. *Can you sometimes be beside each other and sometimes be one behind the other?*
3. *Can you and your partner play your instruments while moving back to back?*
4. *Trade instruments with another set of partners and move again.*

Instrument Alert *(Group)*

Equipment: One instrument per child; use a variety of instruments.

The children sit in a scattered formation. When you call out an instrument the children with that instrument get to move about the room while playing their instrument. It may be helpful for you to play that instrument at the same time. When you call out another instrument the first group needs to stop where they are and sit down. Sometimes it is fun to call **all** instruments. After doing so, give the children until a quick count of five to exchange instruments with someone, and everyone sits down. Start again by calling just one instrument.

Hidden Sounds *(Group)*

Equipment: One triangle, one tambourine, one drum.

Show the children each instrument. Name it and play it. The children then listen to each instrument with their eyes closed. Select three helpers. The chil-

dren again close their eyes while you give each helper one instrument. These three musicians then quietly move to different parts of the room. When you give a signal to one of the musicians, she should play her instrument. The children in the group should listen carefully for the sound. They then open their eyes and move to where they heard the sound. The group then sits down in that spot.

The teacher may select three new musicians, or she may only replace the one who played her instrument. Continue the game until each person gets a turn to be one of the musicians. The game is made more challenging if you use a larger variety of instruments, or use instruments that sound more alike.

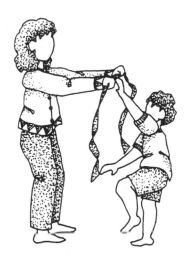

Ribbon Antics

INTRODUCTION

Most streamers or ribbons that can be purchased for rhythm or movement activities are attached to some type of handle, wand, stick, or ball. Do you see the problems already? To relieve the stress of dealing with detached parts, and to prevent the danger of children running with sticks, why not make your own ribbons? The sheerer the fabric, the greater the "twirlability" of the streamer. I once had available some donated fabric that was 42 inches wide from selvage to selvage. Thus was the 42-inch preschool ribbon born. Cut 5-inch-wide strips from selvage to selvage. Fold the strips in half, wrong sides together. Stitch, using a half-inch seam. Turn the strips right-side-out and your ribbon is finished. If the ends are not cut on the selvage it will be necessary to turn the ends under and stitch them. Avoid the hassle and danger of adding handles to the ribbons. Actually, the handles limit the versatility of the streamers, as you will see in the following lessons. Let community organizations or school groups help you with the sewing.

Check your local library or other available media centers for records or tapes you might use in your movement program. Better yet, why not create your own interagency media center? Join with other daycare centers and preschools in your area for the purposes of purchasing and sharing equipment. There are several advantages to this system. First of all, higher volume purchasing is usually treated to bigger discounts. Second, by agreeing to share the equipment with only three other organizations, you can quadruple your spending power overnight. Finally, this increased spending power will immediately enable the children to experience a broader range of activities. Cooperation is continually stressed in the lessons throughout this book. Let's not just teach the children to cooperate. Let's put that concept to work more in our adult world too!

LESSON 1

Ribbon Aerobics (Warm-up)

Equipment: One ribbon per child; lively music.

The children are in a scattered formation. They copy your actions as you lead them in a variety of warm-up movements:

1. *Hold the ribbon in one hand and make big arm circles with that arm. Change hands and do arm circles with the other arm.*
2. *Jog in place while shaking the ribbon with one hand. Keep jogging and change hands.*
3. *Wave the ribbon up and down in front of yourself, going across your body from left to right (or right to left). Make big waves. Change hands.*
4. *Hold the ribbon in front of yourself, one end in each hand. Alternately kick each leg up, trying to kick the ribbon.*
5. *Hold the ribbon in one hand. Hold your arm straight above your head and twirl the ribbon like a lasso. Change hands and repeat.*
6. *Hold one end of the ribbon in each hand. Hold it straight and taut above your head. Jump, doing either a plain jump, jumping jacks and jills, or a stride jump.*

Ribbon Challenges (Individuals)

Equipment: One ribbon per child.

1. *Lay the ribbon flat on the floor. Walk on it as you would walk on a tightrope. Can you go backwards on your tightrope?*

2. *Keep the ribbon flat on the floor. Stand beside the ribbon. Jump back and forth over it.*

3. *Stand behind the ribbon. Can you jump back and forth over it?*

4. *Toss the ribbon up in the air and catch it. Can you do that with your other hand?*

5. *Hold the ribbon up high and twirl in a circle. Can you twirl in the other direction? Stop before you get too dizzy!*

6. *Hold the ribbon high and run with it as if it were a kite. Watch out for each other! Change hands. Can you move some way other than running?*

7. To prepare for the following activity, show the children how to run and leap. Let them practice.

Flashdance Ribbons (Individuals)

Equipment: One ribbon per child; the song "Flashdance." (I use the album *A Thriller For Kids*, by Georgiana Stewart, Kimbo Educational, P.O. Box 477, Long Branch, New Jersey 07740.)

Part	Directions	Count
1	(Hold ribbon in one hand.) *Run and leap.*	4×8
2	*Move sideways with quick, small steps.*	8
	Change directions.	8
	Move in first direction. (Crossing feet is even trickier!)	8
	Change directions.	8
3	(Hold ribbon with two hands in front of yourself.) *Jump and twist hips.*	4×8
4	(Hold ribbon in one hand.) *Swing ribbon in a figure eight pattern in front of yourself.*	2×8
	Change hands and repeat the figure eight pattern.	2×8
	Repeat Parts 1 through 4.	

Runaway Ribbon (Partners)

Equipment: One ribbon for every two children.

The children stay in their self-space for the first part of the activity. One child starts with the ribbon. He squats down and vigorously wiggles the ribbon on the floor. His partner tries to stop the wiggling by stepping on the ribbon. As soon as she steps on the ribbon, it is her turn to be the "wiggler."

Then challenge the children to stop the ribbon by grabbing it with their hand. The wiggler should still keep the ribbon on the floor.

The wiggler is then going to move about the room while wiggling the ribbon on the floor. The chaser follows, trying to step on the ribbon. Trade jobs whenever the ribbon is caught. Remind the children to watch out for each other!

Ribbon Stunts (Partners)

Equipment: One ribbon for every two children.

Each partner holds one end of the ribbon. *Hold the ribbon up high and turn under your upraised arm.* Change hands and try it again. (See "Wring the Dishcloth" activity in Stunts and Tumbling Lesson 1.)

Hold the ribbon lower, about knee-high. Each of you step over the ribbon with one foot, so your back is to your partner. Continue over the ribbon with your other foot so you are back to your starting position. (See "Over The Fence" activity in Stunts and Tumbling Lesson 2.)

Limbo and Leap (Group)

Equipment: One ribbon, or two ribbons tied together for extra length.

You and a helper hold the ribbon straight and taut, at about shoulder-height of the children. The children line up one behind the other and take turns trying to go under the ribbon without touching it. Each time every child has had a turn, lower the ribbon. The children may not be able to do the traditional limbo position, but that's okay. Let them crawl or slide under the ribbon.

Ribbon Tag (Group)

Equipment: One ribbon per child.

Each child tucks the ribbon into her waistband behind her back. The game begins with one chaser (Why not you?) and the other children are all runners. The game is played like tag, but instead of tagging you, the chaser will pull out your ribbon. When your ribbon is pulled, you also become a chaser. Designate a specific spot for the children to place their ribbons when they are pulled. (It is also helpful to talk with the children about the fact that the game is played until everyone becomes a chaser. Point out that *everyone* will get caught and that's okay. *In fact, we hope we can catch everyone, or we will have to stay here all night chasing you . . . and the next night . . . and the next night . . . oh no!*)

Variations

1. Keep only one or two chasers at all times. The two chasers start without ribbons, and when they "catch" someone they get that person's ribbon. The person caught becomes the new chaser.

2. Mark a giant circle in the room. The chaser stays inside the circle. Ribbons can only be pulled when the runners dare to step inside the circle. The game can be played with chasers exchanging places with runners; or it can be played until all of the children are chasers and there is no one left to chase.

Jump and Touch (Group)

Equipment: One ribbon.

Hold one ribbon up high and off to your side. The children form a line one behind the other. They take turns jumping up and trying to touch the ribbon. You can start with the ribbon low and gradually raise it. Or you can alter the height of the ribbon for each individual—so everyone is successful and everyone is challenged!

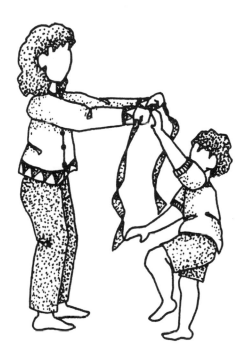

LESSON 2

The following lesson has a somewhat different format than any previous lessons. The following lesson is simply a series of dances I choreographed for young children. Specific directions are given for each part of the dance, and the directions are accompanied by a specific eight-beat/count. The count is for the benefit of the teacher who wants to perform the dance as it is written. But never forget that this book is simply meant to be a "jumping off point," so don't hesitate to create your own movements! If the count is listed as "2 × 8," that means to count to eight twice. With the exception of the first song, all of the music for the "Ribbon Rodeo" is taken from the record album *Disney Pardners* by Walt Disney Productions, Vista Records, Burbank, California 91521.

The Handshake Song (Partners)

Equipment: One ribbon per child.

Formation: Partners facing each other, shaking hands. Tie the ribbon on each child's right wrist.

Part	Directions	Count
	Practice shaking hands. The ribbon indicates the correct hand to use.	
1	*Shake hands while singing:*	
	"Friendship, friendship, Just a perfect blendship."	8
2	*Start with your arms above your head.*	
	Roll your arms down to the floor and back up again.	8
	"When other friendships are all gone, Ours will still be strong."	
3	*Fingers spread wide—jab hands up in the air.*	5
	"Da-da-da da-da"	
4	*Bump your partner's hips.*	3
	"Bump, bump, bump."	
	At the end of the song the children quickly change partners, then start singing again.	

Pecos Bill (Individuals)

Equipment: One ribbon per child; record album *Disney Pardners*; record player.

Formation:	Scattered. Hold each end of the ribbon as if holding the reins of a horse.

Part	Directions	Count
1	*Prance with high steps forward.*	8
	Prance backwards.	8
	Prance forward.	8
	Prance backwards.	8
2	*Stand still. Twirl the ribbon above your head as if twirling a lasso.*	8
	Twirl lasso on left side.	8
	Twirl lasso on right side.	8
	Switch lasso from hand to hand around waist.	8
3	Repeat Parts 1 and 2.	
4	*Hold ribbon with both hands. Bounce your knees and sway lasso left and right.*	2×8
5	Repeat Parts 1 and 2.	
3	Repeat Part 4.	
2	Repeat Part 2.	

A Cowboy Needs a Horse (Partners)

Equipment:	One ribbon per child; record album *Disney Pardners*; record player.
Formation:	Partners. One child holds a ribbon in each hand. *Hold your hands up by your shoulders, with the ribbons behind your back.* This person is the "horse." The "rider" is the other child, who stands behind the "horse," holding the two ribbons as if they were the reins of the horse.

Part	Directions	Count
1	The horse and rider do a slow walk.	8
2	*Stand still and sway to the left and right.*	8
3	*Stand still and dip up and down.*	8

4	The horse and rider switch positions.	
	It is easiest if you just lay the ribbons down, and walk to your new position.	8
5	Repeat Parts 1 through 4	
6	Repeat Parts 1 through 3	

Git Along Little Doggies (Group)

Equipment: One ribbon per child, record album *Disney Pardners*; record player.

Formation: Scattered. Tuck the ribbon into your waistband in back so it represents your calf's tail.

Part	Directions	Count
	Before starting the dance, talk about what a "doggie" is. Ask the children to listen for the "mooing" sounds on the record.	
	While the counts are shown as 8, the beat is counted: "1-and, 2-and, 3-and," etc.	
1	*Gallop about the room.*	2 × 8
2	*Sway your hips so your tail sways.*	2 × 8
3	*Prance about the room.*	2 × 8
4	*Sway your hips, but hold the tail in one hand and swing the tail.*	8
5	Repeat Parts 1 and 2.	

Don't Fence Me In (Group)

Equipment: One ribbon per child; record album *Disney Pardners*; record player.

Formation: The children make a circle around the teacher. You hold one end of each child's ribbon, and the child holds the other end. This links everyone together as in a merry-go-round.

Part	Directions	Count
1	*Walk in a circle.*	2 × 8
2	*Reverse the direction of the circle.*	2 × 8

3   *Bend down low and shake the ribbons.*   8

4   *Stand on tiptoes, hold the ribbons up high overhead and shake them.*   8

5   Repeat Parts 1 through 4.

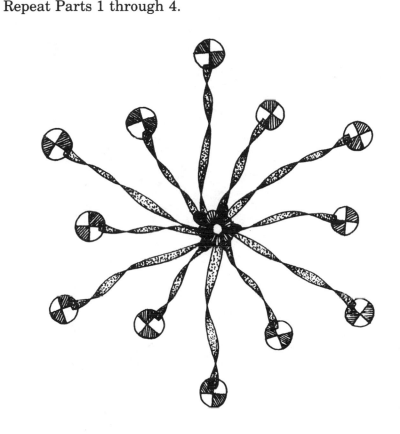

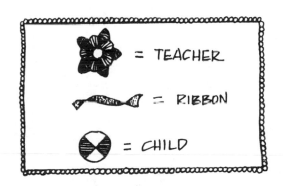

Parachute Activities

INTRODUCTION

Parachute activities provide a wide variety of movement opportunities for children. Some of the activities can be extremely vigorous, and as such they are wonderful for developing shoulder, arm, and hand strength. On the other hand, parachute activities can be slow, gentle, and calming. The parachute also lends itself well to rhythm and dance activities.

While the parachute activities, in general, provide fewer chances for individual exploration, they are wonderful for helping children to learn to work with a group. A frequent change of activities will keep the children involved and enthused; and the vigorous nature of the parachute activities dictates a constant interchange of fast movements with the slower activities.

Parachutes come in various sizes ranging from 6 feet to 42 feet in diameter, with the price range being from approximately $25 to $200. Parachutes can be found in virtually every physical education equipment catalogue. *Real* parachutes used by the armed forces are available for as little as $15 from surplus supply outlets or catalogues.

I have always used one of these real parachutes, and it has proved to be very satisfactory. It is important to remove all of the nylon cords, even those across the center air-release hole. The big drawback to a real parachute is its enormous size. The children will simply have to roll the edges of the parachute until it is the desired size. The parachute can also be cut down to a more manageable size and re-hemmed.

If you have any doubts as to what size parachute to buy, purchase the larger size. A parachute that is too large can always be rolled to a smaller size, whereas a too small parachute is very limiting. Additionally, a full-sized or queen-sized blanket easily replaces a 6-foot parachute. Depending on the size of the group or the specific nature of the activity, in many cases a blanket can be substituted for the parachute.

Parachutes are easily washed and dried, although the larger parachutes require the oversized machines available at laundromats. Should the parachute tear, it is easily repaired with a patch. The patching material does not have to be nylon. A cotton patch larger than the tear can simply be zigzagged onto the parachute fabric. For added durability, place a patch on both sides of the parachute.

Store the parachute by stuffing it into a clean laundry bag or one of the many types of nylon bags available.

LESSON 1

Shake, Shake, and Shake

Equipment: Parachute.

Show the children how to roll the parachute if the parachute is oversized. Check to make sure the children are using the overhand grip.

1. *Everyone together shake the parachute as fast as you can!* This is a very tiring activity. As you see the children tiring, slow the movement. *Everyone together shake the parachute gently.*

2. *Shake the parachute fast again, and this time jump up and down while shaking. Then go slowly.*

3. Point out that the opposite of *fast* is *slow.* Then talk with the children about *big* and *little. Make big, tall waves with the parachute. Your arms will have to go very high and then very low. Now try little waves—make very tiny hand movements to make little waves.* Alternate big and little movements for a couple of turns.

4. If the parachute is multi-colored, let the children holding onto just one color shake the parachute while the others rest. Try having children holding onto just two colors shake the parachute at one time.

5. *How does the parachute move if you move your arms from side to side?*

Merry-Go-Round

Equipment: Parachute.

1. *Everyone hold the parachute and step backwards so the parachute is very taut and up off the floor. Hold the parachute with just one hand and we'll all walk in a circle going left.* (Everyone should be walking forward.)

2. *Now hold the parachute with your other hand, and we'll make our circle go in the other direction.*

3. *Let's go to our left again. This time we'll jog and make our merry-go-round go a bit faster. Switch hands, and we'll make our merry-go-round go in the other direction.*

4. *We'll go left again. Hold the parachute with one hand. Let's try skipping or galloping. Now to the right.*

5. *Hold the parachute with both hands, and face the parachute. Let's all slide sideways to the left to make our merry-go-round go! Now let's go right.*

6. *Can we jump to the left to make the merry-go-round go? Can we jump to the right?*

Tug for Joy

Equipment: Parachute.

1. Instruct the children to pull on the parachute as hard as they can when you give the signal. This is a very tiring activity. Do several repetitions for short bursts of time.
2. *Stand with your back to the parachute. Hold the parachute behind your back. Pull the parachute as hard as you can.*

Under The Big Top

Equipment: Parachute.

One of the great things about working with a parachute is the spirit of cooperation.

1. When the children want to raise the parachute up high, teach them to start by bending over, with the parachute near their ankles. *Count to three together, and on the count of three raise the parachute up high and hold it there.*
2. The children will take turns moving under the parachute while it is raised up high. Caution the children to watch for each other while moving. Call the names of the children who will be moving under the 'chute before raising the parachute. This is an opportunity for the children to explore and move freely.
3. Give the children a second turn to move under the parachute. Talk about the circus—the big tents, the animals, the clowns, and other acts you might see. *Now our parachute is going to be a circus tent. When it is your turn to move under the parachute, will you be a circus animal or a clown?*

Giant Balloon

Equipment: Parachute.

Lay the parachute flat on the floor. Kneel on the parachute, and hold your hands straight up in the air. Then explain to the children that this is the way they will kneel on the parachute after they raise it up.

Start with the parachute down by your ankles. On the count of three raise the parachute up high. I will give a signal; then quickly pull the parachute down to the floor and kneel on it. If this is done correctly you will capture lots of air, so the parachute will be all puffed up.

Talk with the children about what is holding the parachute up. Compare it to filling a balloon with air. Instruct the children to stay in their spaces, but to use their hands to pat the air out of the parachute.

Repeat the activity. As the children are raising the parachute this time, they may want to pretend to be blowing air into the parachute, as if they were blowing up a balloon.

Super Tent

Equipment: Parachute; variety of balls. (Optional: flashlight.)

Talk to the children about camping. Some of the children will have experienced sleeping in a tent, but everyone will be excited to be inside the Super Tent!

1. *The parachute will be blown up just like the Giant Balloon. But when you bring the parachute down, quickly step inside the parachute and sit down on the edge of the parachute!* You may need to practice this once or twice until everyone learns to sit on the parachute. Explain to the children about how important it is to sit on the 'chute so the air doesn't go out. *What happens if the air goes out of the tent? That's right, the tent will fall down!*

2. When everyone is sitting inside the tent, *rock back and forth together. Now rock from side to side.*

3. *Reach up with your arms to pat the ceiling of the tent.*

4. *Lie on your backs* (still on the edge of the 'chute) *and kick the ceiling of the tent. Kick faster!*

5. *Stay in your spot so the tent stays up. Let's try rolling some balls to each other across the floor of the tent.*

6. Darken the room. (Leave a little light on for those non-nocturnal types.) An adult with a flashlight stands on the outside of the parachute. Play the light all about the outside of the 'chute, while encouraging the children on the inside of the tent to watch the firefly as it quickly dances about.

Parachute Popcorn

Equipment: Parachute; ten or more large or small light-weight balls.

The children stand around the parachute, holding it with an overhand grip. Dump all of the balls into the parachute. Tell the children that it is time to make popcorn. The balls are the pieces of popcorn, and if they shake the parachute hard enough, the corn will start to pop.

Keep popping the corn until all of the balls have flown off the parachute. Designate some youngsters to retrieve the balls. Pop the corn again.

Variation: Let the children retrieve the balls as they fly off the parachute. The other children keep popping the corn all the time. *Pop until you're too pooped to pop.*

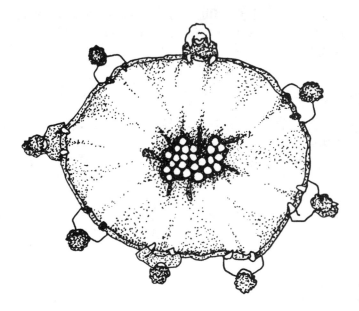

LESSON 2

Jump and 'Chute

Equipment: Parachute; lively music; tape or record player.

The children gather around the parachute and hold on using the overhand grip. Lead the children in a warm-up routine using a variety of movements. Try to alternate leg movements with arm movements. The following are some examples of movements to use. Do several repetitions of each movement.

1. *Jump in place.*
2. *Swing your arms left and right.*
3. *Alternate leg kicks, kicking the bottom of the parachute.*
4. *Move your arms up and down, from head to knees.*
5. *Jump and twist your hips.*
6. *Hold the parachute with one hand; wave the other hand in the air.*
7. *Hop on one foot; hop on the other foot.*

Freeze Shapes

Equipment: Parachute.

The children stand around the parachute, but leave the parachute on the floor. Talk with the children about making their body into a shape and "freezing" their body in that shape. Encourage the children to practice making shapes. When you say "Freeze," they need to freeze their bodies in whatever position

FREEZE!

they are in at that time. When you say "Thaw," the children can move again. Practice several freezes and thaws.

The children now hold the parachute with the overhand grip. Practice counting to three together and then raising the 'chute together. From two to four children at a time will get to make freeze shapes under the parachute. Call the names of the children before raising the parachute. When the others raise the 'chute, the "freeze" children run under the chute. Let the parachute fall gently over them. Then count to three and raise the 'chute again. When you raise the parachute, the children under it will be frozen in their shapes. Let them come out before lowering the parachute. Continue the game until everyone has had a turn to make a freeze shape.

Cooperative Catching

Equipment: Parachute; several large balls.

The children are gathered around the parachute, holding it with an overhand grip. Put one ball into the center of the parachute.

1. *Count to three together and flip the parachute up so the ball flies into the air. Then hold the parachute still, and see if you can catch the ball in it. (This is different than Parachute Popcorn. In that game you keep shaking the parachute so the balls keep flipping up. In this game you do one flip, then stop and catch the balls. Then another flip, and stop and catch the balls, etc.)*

2. *Add more balls to the parachute. Each time you catch the balls, count them to see how many are left. Keep tossing and catching until there are none left to catch.*

3. Experiment with the children. *Is it easier to catch the balls if we don't toss them so high? Are the balls more likely to "fly away" if we toss them really high?*

Parachute Golf

Equipment: Parachute with a hole in the middle; several tennis balls or plastic golf balls.

The children are gathered around the parachute, holding it with an overhand grip. The object of this game is to gently roll a tennis ball (or plastic golf ball) around on the parachute, trying to get it to fall through the hole in the middle of the parachute. Encourage the children to gently raise and lower the parachute, rather than to shake it to get the ball to fall through.

Start the ball on the edge of the parachute. Never start it in the same place twice.

Pop Goes the Weasel

Equipment: Parachute. (Optional: tape or record of the song "Pop Goes The Weasel"; tape or record player.)

Children are gathered around the parachute, facing counterclockwise and holding the 'chute with their inside hands. If the children do not already know it, teach them the song "Pop Goes The Weasel." The children walk in a counterclockwise circle as they sing "Pop Goes The Weasel."

All around the cobbler's bench
The monkey chased the weasel,
The monkey thought 'twas all in fun,
Pop goes the weasel.

When the children sing the word "Pop," they stop walking and quickly raise (pop) the parachute.

Walk in the opposite direction for the next verse:

A penny for a spool of thread,
A penny for a needle,
That's the way the money goes,
Pop goes the weasel.

Keep repeating the verses and changing directions with each verse.

Variations:

1. A few children at a time can be crouched down under the parachute. They can pop up when the parachute is popped up.

2. Use a record or a tape of "Pop Goes The Weasel" instead of singing the song.

Bean Soup

Equipment: Parachute; one beanbag per child.

1. The children are gathered around the parachute, holding it with an overhand grip. Place a beanbag on the parachute in front of each child.

2. When you give the "Go" signal, the children begin shaking the parachute very vigorously. They are trying to shake the beanbags into the middle of the parachute, thereby making bean soup. (If the parachute has a hole in the middle, continue shaking until all of the beanbags have fallen through the hole.)

The beanbags actually make the parachute quite a bit heavier for the children, so this is a good workout. Another way to get the beanbags to the middle is to raise the outer edge of the parachute. This causes the bags to slide into the middle. The children can all do this together, or they can take turns sliding their beanbags to the middle. Individual turns allow the children to watch the beanbags slide down the 'chute and into the bean pot.

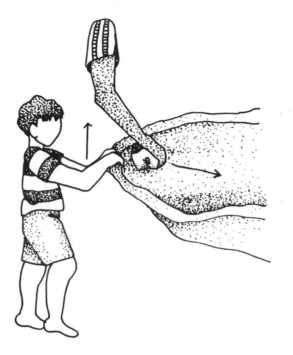

London Bridge

Equipment: Parachute.

The children sit around the parachute. Teach them the words to the song "London Bridge":

London Bridge is falling down,
Falling down, falling down.
London Bridge is falling down,
My fair lady.

Select pairs of children to gallop or skip under the parachute while the others hold the parachute aloft. Depending on the size of the group and the size of the parachute, let one, two, or three pairs go under the 'chute at one time. The pairs should line up behind each other and gallop under the parachute from one end of the parachute to the other. When they get to the far end of the parachute, they go out from under the 'chute and gallop around the outside of the circle back to the London Bridge entrance. When the words "My fair lady" are sung, the parachute holders gently bring the 'chute down over anyone who is under the parachute.

The parachute holders raise the parachute while singing the second verse:

Build it up with iron bars,
Iron bars, iron bars.
Build it up with iron bars,
My fair lady.

After the children have sung the two verses while lowering and then raising the parachute, select other pairs to go under London Bridge.

Variation: The same pairs keep going under London Bridge until they are caught by the parachute.

LESSON 3

Parachute Rides

Equipment: Parachute; wide-open play area (outdoors is ideal, but carefully inspect the grass for foreign objects.)

1. Lay the parachute on the ground. (If you are indoors on a tile floor, advise the children not to walk across the parachute, since it will be very slippery.) Divide the class into groups of six or eight. The groups will take turns giving individuals in their groups rides on the parachute.

2. The rider lies down on the back end of the parachute. The pullers are at the front of the parachute, helping the teacher to pull the parachute. Half of the pullers should stand on one side of the teacher, with the other half on the other side of the teacher. Run together to give the rider an exciting ride on the parachute. It may even be possible to pull two children at once.

3. Then give another group a chance to pull one of their group members. This gives the first group a chance to rest, as pulling is strenuous work.

Variation: If you are outdoors and there is some wind, pull the riders with the wind at your back. After pulling for some distance, have the rider get off the parachute. All of the children run around to the back end of the parachute, lift it off the ground and run into the wind. The parachute will billow in the wind like a giant kite.

Ocean Waves

Equipment: Parachute; grassy or carpeted area.

The children are gathered around the parachute, holding it with an overhand grip. The children vigorously shake the parachute, using large up-and-down arm movements. Appoint two or three children at a time to walk on the parachute while the others are making waves. Encourage the children to walk near the outer edges of the parachute, for the larger waves can be found there.

Safety note: It is safer if the children all move in the same direction while walking or running on the parachute. Some of the waves are so big it is difficult for the children to see each other. Also, it is very important that this not be done on a tile or wooden floor: these surfaces are too slippery.

We Can Fly!

Equipment: Parachute; wide-open space (outdoors is ideal).

Lay the parachute flat on the ground. Divide the class into groups of six or eight. The groups will take turns flying the parachute across the field. All of the children in the group need to stand at one end of the parachute. They can grip the parachute with one or two hands. On a signal from the teacher, the children take off running across the field. The teacher may want to position herself in the middle of the runners, so she can control their speed.

If doing this activity outdoors, it is best to run into the wind with the parachute. This causes the parachute to billow in the wind.

Under the Ocean

Equipment: Parachute.

1. The children are gathered around the parachute, holding it with an overhand grip at about waist height.

2. Name two or three children at a time to crawl under the parachute while the parachute is held still. Continue until every child has a turn to crawl around under the parachute.

3. Then give each child a second turn, but this time the ocean will be full of waves. The children hold the parachute waist high or lower, and they shake the parachute to create ocean waves. Continue until all those who want a turn are able to crawl under the ocean waves.

Variation: Hold the parachute still, with no shaking. As the children crawl under the parachute, *slowly* lower it to the floor. When the parachute is touching the crawlers, that is their signal to crawl to the edge of the parachute and come out from under it.

Parachute Exercises

Equipment: Parachute.

Lay the parachute out flat on the floor. The children sit around the parachute. The children put their legs under the parachute so their legs are completely covered.

1. *Hold on to the edge of the parachute. Bend your knees so your knees are sticking up under the parachute. Keep holding the parachute and alternately straighten and bend knees. Go as fast as you can.*
2. *Sit with your knees bent and your legs still under the parachute. Lie down. Sit up.*
3. *Roll the edge of the parachute towards the center of the 'chute. Now lie down and sit up.* (As the children roll the parachute in, it will help them to sit up.)
4. *Do several repetitions. Roll the parachute again and repeat the sit-ups.*
5. *While sitting and holding the parachute, raise your arms up and down. You can also do one arm at a time.*

Snake in the Grass

Equipment: Parachute; grassy or carpeted surface.

Lay the parachute flat on the grass. Be sure to carefully inspect the grass under the 'chute for any foreign objects. You are the snake, and you lie down on your stomach in the center of the parachute. The children are standing on the parachute at random. They are free to walk all about on the parachute, but they must not get off the parachute. The snake crawls on his tummy, trying to tag the children. Any children tagged must become a snake also. Continue the game until all of the children have become snakes.

Special Days and Seasons

INTRODUCTION

The following material is for use on holidays, special days, or for activities linked to specific seasons of the year. While most of the equipment needs can be met with the previously accumulated equipment, there are also some special equipment requirements. However, these are easily accessible common household items or items that can be readily made.

A garden hose is a very useful item for Fire Prevention Week. To make it safer for the children to use, however, wrap both ends in masking tape or duct tape. If two hoses are connected, wrap the connection in tape also.

Fire engine steering wheels can be made from the plastic lids that go with the plastic ice cream buckets or containers. To make different colors of steering wheels, cut a circle of construction paper the same size as the lid and tape it to the lid. (You can cover both sides of the lid.)

The fire fighter clothes can be regular adult-sized clothing items, but use only old clothes in case of damage. The plastic ice cream buckets can be substituted for fire fighter hats, but be sure to remove any handles on the buckets.

One of the most enjoyable pieces of equipment is the jack o' lantern ball. Use 6-inch to 8½-inch soft rubber balls that are used for the Large Ball Activities. Make jack o' lantern faces on the balls using black electrician's tape or black plastic tape. Use your imagination! When you first use the balls (nicknamed "jack o' balls"), challenge the children to find the eyes, the nose, and the mouth.

The "Trick or Treat" game is more fun if a variety of objects are used, instead of just the beanbags. Pull out a variety of objects from the equipment closet, such as tennis balls, plastic lids, ribbons, scarves, small pieces of rubber band rope, plastic scoops, and so on. Or, use small manipulatives from the classroom. Try to have the same items for each group.

A black plastic cauldron is fun for many Halloween activities. They are readily available at local discount stores. One could be made, however, by covering a box or a bucket with black paper.

Halloween is the perfect time of the year to purchase masks, which can be turned into blindfolds. Purchase the half-masks, which cover only the eyes and the top of the nose. Cover the eye openings on both sides with duct tape, and you have very effective, easy-to-use blindfolds.

Construction paper cutouts can be used as props for a variety of activities. In many cases, the movement activity can be coordinated with a coloring and cutting activity by having the children color and cut out the items needed. In some cases, there may be cookie cutters which are the appropriate shape, so children may trace the shape, then color and cut it. An alternative is for you to make the shapes. Then it would be advisable to laminate the cut-outs to lengthen their life.

The "food" items needed for the "Harvest Game" can likewise be made by the children. Or they might be found in the housekeeping or grocery store section of the classroom.

Sleigh bells can be purchased at discount stores. They can also be made by sewing bells onto one of the dance ribbons.

Solicit "ice skating" socks from parents. Everyone has old sweat socks, gym socks, or tube socks just waiting for a new use.

Local businesses and corporations can be an excellent source of recycled computer paper. End rolls of newsprint can also be found (or purchased for a nominal fee) at local newspaper offices.

Carpet squares are a staple of preschool equipment. Any store selling floor coverings will have the samples. There may be a nominal fee, but the samples last forever.

Old or damaged bicycle inner tubes or tires are readily available at bicycle repair shops. These shops will be more than happy to have you carry away the old tubes. Be sure to cut the valves out of the tubes.

Parachutes are described in the Parachute Activities section.

Valentines are frequently donated *after* Valentine's Day. Plan ahead, and there will be plenty of valentines for the games and activities. Some of the valentines can be laminated and saved for future use.

Plastic Easter eggs can be purchased very reasonably at discount stores. Easter eggs can be made, however, using the "eggs" in which some hosiery is packaged. These eggs can be decorated with stickers.

A really fun piece of equipment is the dyed Easter egg ball. Tennis balls can be dyed using food coloring or packaged Easter egg dye. Prepare the dye as directed. Circles of color can be put on the ball by partially submerging the ball in the dye. The farther the ball is dipped into the dye, the bigger the circle of color. Other designs can be made on the balls using masking tape. The tape can be cut into quarter-inch or half-inch strips and wound randomly around the ball. Completely submerge the ball in the dye for several minutes. When the ball is dry, remove the tape. Tape can be put on the ball in any kind of shape. After the ball is dyed, the shape will appear in the original color of the ball.

The ribbons used in many of the activities are described in the section on Rhythm and Dance Activities. The buckets are described more fully in the section on Small Balls and Buckets.

The majority of the activities in this section are group activities. However, each lesson is always started with warm-up or individual activities. The children need this opportunity to move and explore.

Fire Prevention Week

LESSON 1

Fire Fighter Exercises (Warm-up)

Equipment: Garden hose (or long jump rope to simulate a fire fighter hose).

Lay the fire hose on the floor in a straight line. Each child finds a place to hold onto the hose. On the signal from the Fire Chief, the children practice raising and lowering the hose together. The Fire Chief gives signals so the children quickly touch the hose:

1. *To your toes*
2. *To your knees*
3. *To your tummy*
4. *To your chin*
5. *Above your head*

Repeat the calls several times.

Lay the fire hose on the floor in a straight line. Each child finds a space to stand beside the hose. The "fire fighters" limber up by jumping sideways over the hose. Have the children jump back and forth several times, always trying to jump faster.

Fire Hose Shake (Group)

Equipment: Garden hose (or long jump rope to simulate a fire hose).

The children will all be fire fighters. They line up alongside the fire hose, then pick it up and carry it near their tummies. The fire fighters move together, carrying the fire hose all about the room. The fire fighters can move several ways:

1. Walking forward
2. Walking backwards
3. Galloping
4. Sliding sideways
5. Walking on tiptoes

Of course, the real fun is stopping frequently to put out a "fire." The Fire Chief should explain beforehand that real fire hoses are much bigger, and when the water comes out of the hose it is very strong and powerful. So when the fire fighters are using the hose to put out a fire, they probably shake all over!

The Fire Chief may want to start the game by appointing herself the one who finds the fires. However, the more enthusiastic fire fighters will soon be finding fires everywhere! The Fire Chief can also have the fire fighters at the front of the hose move to the back after every fire.

Find the Fire! (Group)

Equipment: 1 carpet square per child.

This is a game which requires the children to use auditory discrimination. Designate a certain area of the room as the Fire Station. Give each child a

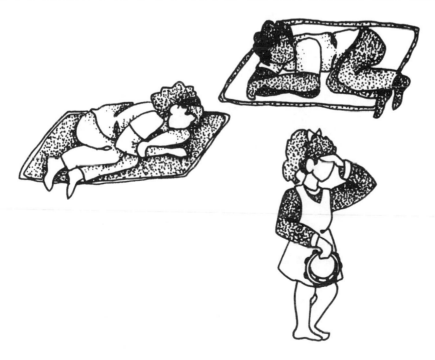

carpet square to lie on, as you explain that each fire fighter has a bed at the Fire Station.

Each fire fighter is to lie down, close his eyes, and "go to sleep." While the fire fighters are sleeping, the Fire Chief will go out and watch for fires. When the Fire Chief spots a fire, she yells, "Fire! Fire! Fire!" The fire fighters then jump up out of bed and run to where the Fire Chief is standing.

The Fire Chief does not need to hide in the room, but she should change locations each time before she yells "Fire!" The challenge is for the "sleeping" fire fighters to locate the Fire Chief by listening to her voice. It is an even greater challenge if there is more than one Fire Chief. Each Chief stands in a different part of the room, and when one of the Chiefs yells "Fire!", the children have to distinguish which Chief was yelling and run to that Chief.

It is still a different challenge if each Fire Chief has a different musical instrument, such as a cymbal, tambourine, drum, or triangle, that she plays instead of yelling "Fire!"

After each fire, you may indicate to the fire fighters how they should move as they travel back to the Fire Station: galloping, jumping, or walking backwards, for example.

Fire Truck Drivers (Group)

Equipment: Colored spot markers or plastic lids covered with various colors of construction paper, one for each child.

This is a color differentiation game. The spot markers are the steering wheels of the fire trucks, so each child has his own truck to drive. The truck drivers all line up side by side, ready to drive out of the Fire Station when they are called.

You are the Fire Chief. You move to another area of the room and call, "Fire! Fire! Calling all yellow fire trucks!" All of the children with a yellow steering wheel need to quickly "drive their trucks" (run) to the spot where the

Fire Chief is standing. The yellow fire trucks now stay at their new location. The Fire Chief moves to another area of the room before calling another color.

Vary the sequence in which the colors are called. Each group will always start from its new location. Sometimes call all of the colors at the same time. Encourage the truck drivers to use their sirens!

After the children have played for a short while, encourage the children to trade colors of steering wheels.

> **Variation:** Each fire truck group returns to the Fire Station after each trip to put out a fire.

LESSON 2

Fire Hose Toes (Warm-up)

Equipment: Garden hose.

Lay the hose on the floor in the shape of a circle. The children stand around the hose, facing the inside of the circle. The children should stand with their toes on the hose and their heels on the floor. You lead the children in the following exercise: *Raise your arms up and stand on your tiptoes on the hose. Now bring your arms down and put your heels on the floor.* Repeat this several times. *Can you do this standing on one foot?*

Grip Tight (Warm-up)

Equipment: Garden hose.

Lay the hose on the floor in the shape of a circle. The children stand around the hose, facing the inside of the circle. The children work together to pick up the hose and hold it against their tummies. When you say "Squeeze," the children should squeeze the hose as hard as possible for 3 to 5 seconds. Repeat a few times.

Vary the positions in which the children hold the hose, such as above their heads, down by their toes, and behind their backs. With each position change, do a couple of "squeeze" repetitions.

Variation: Let the children squeeze using only one hand at a time.

Fire Hose Balance (Warm-up)

Equipment: One or two garden hoses.

Lay the hose on the floor in the shape of a circle. The children walk on the hose as if it were a balance beam. Most children will be able to move by putting one foot in front of the other, but others will choose to go sideways. An even greater challenge will be to move backwards.

Fire Engines (Groups)

Equipment: None.

Form fire engines by having groups of three or four children line up one behind the other, each person holding onto the waist of the person in front of her.

Direct the Fire Engines to move certain ways:

1. Forward
2. Backwards

3. Sideways
4. Galloping
5. Walking on tiptoes

After a certain period of time, have the front person in each group go to the back of her Fire Engine. The next person in each line will be the new leader.

After the children become proficient at moving together, hook one or two Fire Engines together. Then challenge the children to move in a variety of ways.

Variation: Four- and five-year-olds will enjoy playing Fire Engine Tag. There should be several Fire Engines, as in the game above, but there also needs to be one or more individuals not connected to any fire engine. These individuals are the Chasers. The Chasers attempt to tag or catch on to the back of any Fire Engine. If a Chaser catches on to the back of a Fire Engine, then the *front* person of that Fire Engine must disconnect and become the new Chaser.

Dress the Fire Fighter! (Groups)

Equipment: Three or four sets of Fire Fighter clothes:

• Adult-sized slacks or jeans
• Adult-sized snowboots
• Adult-sized jackets or long-sleeved shirts
• Plastic fire hats (or ice cream buckets)

The great thing about this activity is that it gives the children practice in getting dressed quickly, and what parent wouldn't love that! Preschoolers are a little young to appreciate a relay as we know it. But they are thrilled if they each get a turn to put on the Fire Fighter clothes and run to put out the fire.

The game moves faster if three or four children can have a turn at the same time. Divide the class into three or four groups, with one child from each group taking a turn at the same time. Each group has one set of Fire Fighter clothes. The object of the game is to put on the clothes as fast as possible, run to a certain point to put out a fire, and run back to the starting point.

The focus of the game should not be on winning, but on:

1. Hurrying
2. Helping (The children naturally seem to start helping each other.)
3. Shouting encouragement

Fire Fighter, Fire Fighter, Fire Chief! (Group)

Equipment: None.

Substitute the words "Fire Fighter" for the word "duck," and the words "Fire Chief" for "goose." Play a Fire Prevention Week version of that age-old favorite "Duck, Duck Goose."

Halloween

LESSON 1

Halloween Mime (Warm-up)

Equipment: None.

Children enjoy acting out various characters and animals from Halloween: bats, witches, ghosts, spiders, cats, and so on.

Black Cats

Start on your hands and knees. Arch your back like a black cat; it will help if you pull your tummy in. Then sag your back so there is a hollow space in your lower back; it will help if you push your tummy towards the floor.

Another way to arch the cat's back is to push yourself up on your toes with your seat in the air. Then go back down on your knees.

Bats

Spread your wings and fly about the room. Remember to watch out for the other bats! When I give the signal, fold your wings and crouch down low. Try flying backwards and sideways also.

Spiders

Spiders scamper across the floor very quickly. Hold yourself up on your hands and feet, and scamper in every direction.

Ghosts

Ghosts move by floating. Move slowly about the room, as if you are floating. Can you float by leaping? Remember to move slowly.

Pumpkin Pass (Groups)

Equipment: Three or four jack o' lantern balls (or pumpkins).

Divide the class into three or four groups. Each group lines up one behind the other. Each group needs one jack o' lantern.

The first person in each group has the jack o' lantern. She passes it over her head to the person behind her. The ball is passed over each person's head in turn, until it reaches the end of the line. The last person in line then runs to the front of the line with the jack o' lantern, and the passing starts all over again.

Variation: The jack o' lantern is passed through the legs of each child, instead of over his head.

Trick or Treat (Groups)

Equipment: Four grocery bags; sixteen bike inner tubes (or hula hoops); sixteen beanbags (or a variety of small objects); four spot markers.

Divide the class into four groups. Each group lines up behind one of the spot markers. In front of each group is a row of four inner tubes, each tube placed about three giant steps ahead of the next one. Place one beanbag inside each inner tube. (Since this is all about trick or treating, a variety of small objects makes the game more exciting.)

The first person in each group is given a sack. She is to go trick or treating by picking up each object in her row. Then she needs to quickly run back to her group and empty her sack. Before the second person takes his turn, the first person needs to replace the objects in the inner tubes.

Variation: Randomly scatter a variety of colored spots about the room. Use two, three, or four different colors. One person will trick or treat at all of the yellow spots, another will trick or treat

at the orange spots, another at the red spots, and another at the green spots. The scattered formation of the spots makes this much more challenging. With a little practice, however, four- and five-year-olds can handle this activity.

Boiling Cauldron (Group)

Equipment: One black plastic cauldron (or a bucket covered with black paper).

The children sit in a circle. Tell them a story about a witch boiling a mysterious brew. As you tell the story, scatter a variety of objects all about the room.

When you give the signal, the children run to pick up all of the objects and fill the cauldron. Remind the children not to touch the cauldron because it is "boiling hot."

The activity can then continue with the children moving about the room in the manner indicated. While the children are moving, you will once again scatter the objects all about the room. The children now need to listen for the special signal (such as "witch's brew") that tells them to once again fill the cauldron. Encourage the children to only take one object at a time to the cauldron.

Pumpkin Face (Group)

Equipment: One or more large drawings of a pumpkin; several smaller pieces that will be the eyes, nose, and mouths of the pumpkins; one or more blindfolds.

The large pumpkin drawings can either be laid flat on the floor or hung on the wall. The children will take turns being blindfolded and positioning a piece on the pumpkin face. Add some unusual pieces, such as eyebrows, ears, individual teeth, or even a beard or a hat.

It would be ideal to have enough large pumpkins so that individual pieces number the same as the number of children. Then the large pumpkin drawings can become part of the Halloween decorations in the classroom.

Pot of Treats

Equipment: One witch's pot; as many beanbags as possible, boundary markers or tape for marking a *big* circle.

You assume the part of the witch and stand inside the big circle. You have inside the circle with you a cauldron full of treats (beanbags). The children try to get the beanbags out of the pot without the witch catching them. They can only be caught when they are inside the circle and holding a beanbag. If a child is caught while holding a beanbag, he must put the beanbag back into the cauldron. It would be helpful to designate an area outside the circle where the children can leave the beanbags.

Some children may want a turn to be the witch inside the circle. Let two or three children be witches at the same time.

LESSON 2

Costumes Alive (Warm-up)

Equipment: None.

The children will enjoy telling about their own Halloween costumes. Encourage them to act out each character as the costume is named.

The children then can work with a partner. The partners take turns acting out a Halloween character, while their partner tries to guess the character.

Pumpkin Patch (Individuals)

Equipment: One jack o' lantern ball for each child.

The children are in scattered formation, each holding a jack o' lantern ball.

1. Ask the children to really look at their own ball. *Does it look happy, sad, scary, or mad? Can you make your own face look like the jack o' lantern's?*

2. *Put your pumpkin on the floor. Now, imagine that we are all standing in the pumpkin patch. Imagine that you have found the biggest pumpkin in the patch. Pick the pumpkin up as if it were really very heavy. Can you walk and carry that heavy, heavy pumpkin without dropping it?*

3. *Gently put that pumpkin on the ground. Now, it is still very heavy. Can you slowly roll that pumpkin around the pumpkin patch?*

4. *Leave the pumpkins on the floor. Very carefully move about the room, being careful not to step on a pumpkin. Move very slowly. When I give the signal, "Boo!", crouch down by the nearest pumpkin. Then make your face look like that jack o' lantern's face.*

Encourage the children to move a variety of ways in the pumpkin patch, sometimes carrying the pumpkin with them, and sometimes leaving the pumpkins in the pumpkin patch. Sometimes the pumpkins are very heavy, and sometimes they are very light.

Spooking Time (Group)

Equipment: Four markers (or plastic jugs) to indicate two lines at opposite ends of a room or playing field.

All of the children stand at one end of the room. You start the game as the "witch," standing in the middle of the room.

The children ask the witch: What time is it?" The witch answers by naming a time, such as "three o'clock." The children keep asking the witch the time until the witch answers, "It's midnight!" When the witch gives the "midnight" answer, the children must run to the other side of the room. The witch tries to tag as many children as possible. Those tagged must stay in the middle with the witch and help to tag the next runners. When there is more than one person in the middle, then the first person who was the witch should give the time. The game continues until everyone has been tagged and is in the middle.

Witch's House (Group)

Equipment: One plastic cauldron (or bucket); one spot marker for each child; chalk; at least one beanbag (or other trick-or-treat object) for each child.

Use the chalk to draw a witch's hat on the back of several of the spot markers. Randomly scatter all of the spots about the playing area. The witch's hat drawings should be on the bottom of each spot, so that they cannot be seen by the children. Place the cauldron in the middle of the playing area.

The spots represent the houses where the boys and girls will go trick-or-treating. Each child will carry a beanbag (this represents their treat). The children move about the playing area in the manner indicated—walking, galloping, tiptoeing, and so on.

When you give the signal, "It's midnight! Run home! Run home!" the children run and stand on any spot. After every child is standing on a spot, instruct them to turn their spot over and look at the bottom. Any child who has a witch's hat on the bottom of his spot has to put his treat (beanbag) in the witch's pot, for he has accidentally run to the witch's house.

There should be extra beanbags, so those who lost their treats to the witch will have a treat for their next turn. As the children are moving again, quickly rearrange the spots so no one knows where the witches' houses are located.

Giant Pumpkin (Group)

Equipment: Two or three large jack o' lantern leaf bags stuffed with newspaper (or two or three of the biggest balls available).

Divide the class into groups according to the number of large jack o' lanterns available. Each group lines up one behind the other at one end of the room.

The first person in each line rolls her giant pumpkin across the room to a certain spot, then back again to her own line. The next person in line then takes his turn. Continue the game until everyone in each line has had a turn.

Variation: The first two or three people in each line have to *carry* the pumpkin across the room and back again.

Thanksgiving

LESSON 1

Turkey in the Straw (Warm-up)

Equipment: Tape or record of "Turkey in the Straw"; tape or record player.

Show the children how to strut like a turkey, sticking their heads out and pulling them in. They can make wings by folding their arms so their hands are tucked up underneath their armpits. Show the children how turkeys sleep (with their heads tucked under their wings).

Play the song "Turkey In The Straw." During the chorus the "turkeys" should proudly strut, sticking their necks out and gobbling. During the verses, the turkeys should crouch down to sleep, tucking their heads under their wings.

Turkey Farmer (Group)

Equipment: An area of the room needs to be designated as the turkey pen. All of the children need to fit comfortably into this area. Tumbling mats can be used, or the area can be marked with spot markers.

Designate yourself as the farmer and have all of the children gather in the turkey pen. The farmer then tells the children that they are *Thanksgiving turkeys* and they are to stay in the pen. Build this up so the children realize that they *should* try to sneak out of the pen as soon as the farmer goes to sleep.

After you have warned the turkeys at length about staying in the turkey pen, you should wander across the room, pretend to do farm work for a short while, and then sit down and fall asleep. After the farmer falls asleep, the turkeys

sneak out of the pen and strut around the barnyard. The farmer, upon awaking, jumps up and proceeds to "shoo" the turkeys into the pen.

The farmer may pretend to lock the gate or pound extra boards across the gate after he gets all of the turkeys into the pen. Continue the game until you can no longer get the turkeys back into the pen.

> **Variation:** The children may take turns being the farmer. In that case, there may be more than one farmer at a time.

Turkey Tag (Group)

> **Equipment:** Construction paper cutouts of turkeys in a variety of two to four colors; one turkey per child; line markers at both ends of the room; masking tape.

Each child tapes a construction paper turkey to his chest. The children line up side by side on a line at one end of the room. You (or a designated child) are the farmer and stand in the middle of the room.

The farmer points out that he is looking for a juicy Thanksgiving turkey. When the farmer calls a certain color of turkey, those children wearing that color of construction paper turkey must run to the line at the other side of the room. If any turkey is tagged, she must join the farmer in helping to tag other turkeys. Continue the game until every turkey is tagged.

Turkey Feathers (Group)

> **Equipment:** One ribbon per child; a small area of the room designated as a turkey pen; (optional: spot markers; a real turkey feather).

If you can, show the children what a real turkey feather looks like. Then give each child a ribbon. The children tuck their ribbon into the back of their waistband. The children are "turkeys," and the ribbon is their turkey feather. The turkeys strut proudly all about the "farm," but they are always watching out for the farmer (you) at Thanksgiving time.

When the farmer shouts "Thanksgiving!" the turkeys must run from the farmer, who is trying to pull each turkey's tail feather. If the turkey's tail feather is pulled, the turkey must go to the turkey pen for one turn. One way for the turkeys to be safe from the farmer is for them to squat down and tuck their heads under their wings.

Variations:

1. The children may take turns being the farmer. In this case, use more than one farmer at a time.
2. Put several spot markers on the floor. The turkeys can be safe by squatting on a spot marker. There should only be a few spot markers on the floor, however, so the turkeys will need to take turns being on and off the markers.

Harvest Game (Group)

Equipment: Four each of construction paper cutouts of a pumpkin, an ear of corn, a tomato, a carrot, an onion, a green pepper, or any other garden vegetables; four plastic buckets; two construction paper circles of each of the following colors: red, blue, green, and yellow; masking tape.

Divide the class into four groups. Have each group sit in a certain spot in the room, with that spot designated by one of the construction paper circles. Each group is going to be called a "family," and this spot will be their "home." Each group is given one plastic bucket, and that bucket has the same color circle taped to it.

The teacher will show the children each of the garden vegetables so they can later recognize them. The teacher then proceeds to "plant" these vegetables in a row at one end of the room. (If there are four groups, the teacher should plant four pumpkins, and so on.) One of the children from each group is given the harvest bucket to carry, but *all* of the children move about the room. When the teacher declares "Harvest Time!" the children with the harvest buckets must run to the garden and pick the one vegetable the teacher tells them to pick. They then carry this bucket back to their "home," where all of the other children have gone to wait.

Continue the game until every child gets to harvest at least one vegetable. Remind the children to stay out of the vegetable garden while they are moving about the room.

Variation: There could be one of each vegetable for each child. Then each child would carry a bucket as they move about the room. When the teacher gives the "Harvest Time" signal, each child selects that vegetable from the garden.

For either version of the game, it becomes more of a memory game if you announce which vegetable to harvest *before* the children begin moving about the room.

At the end of the game, you can ask each child to hold up a certain vegetable, as a way of reviewing the names of the vegetables.

Winter and Christmas

LESSON 1

Reindeer on the Roof (Individuals)

Equipment: None (Optional: sleigh bells).

1. *Imagine that you are a reindeer. Let's see your antlers. Are you proud because you get to help pull Santa's sleigh? Let's see you walk proudly.* Encourage the reindeer to prance all about, walking lightly in the snow.
2. *How would a reindeer walk if the sleigh was loaded with presents and was very heavy?*
3. *Can you move like a reindeer and have your nose flash like Rudolph's at the same time?* (Make your nose flash by holding your hand in front of your nose and opening and closing your fist.)
4. *What if the reindeer were in a big hurry? Can you gallop? Can you gallop with a flashing nose?*
5. *Can you start galloping, and then go faster and faster until you are flying through the sky like Santa's reindeer?*
6. *Now let's see you land on a rooftop. How would you stand if you were afraid of being up so high? What would happen if the rooftop were very slippery?*

Option: Ring sleigh bells whenever the children are moving like reindeer.

The Prancing and Pawing of So Many Hoofs (Partners)

Equipment: None. (Optional: sleigh bells.)

1. *Try moving with a partner reindeer. Stand side by side and hold hoofs. Try prancing, then galloping, and then flying.*
2. *Try moving with one reindeer in front of the other. The back reindeer should hold onto the waist of the front reindeer. Can you prance? Can you prance backwards? Can the two of you pull a very heavy sleigh together?*

Option: Ring sleigh bells while the children are moving like reindeer.

Variation: (For four- and five-year-olds.) Connect two pairs of reindeer together. Two reindeer stand side by side and hold inside hands. Another pair stands behind them. The front and back

230

people on each side connect to each other with their outside hands or with ribbons. The foursome tries to move about the room together. Encourage the children to move in different ways: forward, backwards, sideways, slowly with a heavy load, and so forth.

Ice Skating (Individuals)

Equipment: Two old socks or two beanbags per child. (This activity will not work on a carpeted floor.)

Depending on the size of the socks, the children may need to remove their shoes for this activity. They should, however, keep their own socks on their feet. Simply have them put the old socks over their own. Talk to the children about ice skating on a brisk winter day.

1. *We are now going together to the ice skating rink. As you start to skate, simply slide your feet along the floor.*
2. *Do any of you think you can skate backwards? Remember to just keep sliding your feet.*
3. *Can anyone balance on one ice skate? Can you balance on the other ice skate?*
4. *Can you skate and do a fancy turn?*
5. *Try skating with a partner.*

Variation: If you do not have socks for everyone, simply give each child two beanbags. (Partners can share beanbags and take turns skating.) The children ice skate by putting a beanbag under each foot and sliding along on the beanbags.

The Snowsuit (Group)

Equipment: The book *Thomas' Snowsuit* by Robert N. Munsch and Michael Martchenko. (Ontario: Annick Press, 1985.)

How many of you like to get all dressed in your winter coat, snowpants, snowboots, hats, and mittens so you can go outside to play in the snow? Now that winter is here, let's practice getting dressed in all of our winter gear.

1. *First let's put on our snowsuits (or our snowpants). Sit down, put your feet in, and pull the snowsuit up over your legs. Now stand up, pull the snowsuit up, and put your arms in, one at a time.*

2. *Slowly zip up the snowsuit. Oh, oh, my zipper got stuck! Gently nudge and tug on the zipper, zip it down, and now zip it all the way up. Watch your chin!*

3. *Let's put on our snow boots. Do you like to sit down or stand up? Mine fit kind of tight, and I always have to stamp to get them all the way on.*

4. *And we can finish with our hat and mittens. Does anyone like to wear gloves? Can you get each finger in the right spot?*

Now that you're all dressed in your snowsuits, I'd like to read you the story of Thomas' Snowsuit. *Listen to see if this little boy likes to put on his snowsuit.* Read the story with much expression and lots of theatrics. Encourage the children to join in whenever Thomas emphatically says "Nnnnno!" When individuals scuffle, the children may act that out *individually.*

Snowballs (Group)

Equipment: Lots of sheets of scrap paper, at least 8½ inches by 11 inches. (Recycled computer paper or newspaper is usually readily available.) Tumblings mats are optional.

The children work together to wad up the pieces of paper to make snowballs. Before the children start throwing the snowballs, work out a "stop" signal. When you give the "go" signal, the children begin throwing the snowballs at one another at random.

Tumbling mats can be set up as barriers for the children to hide behind. Then two teams can be organized, with one team on each side of the tumbling mats.

LESSON 2

Ho! Ho! Ho! (Individuals)

Equipment: None.

Encourage the children to act out the following characteristics of Santa Claus:

1. *He has a little round belly that shakes when he laughs "like a bowl full of jelly."*
2. *Santa is very jolly.*
3. *How would Santa walk with a sack full of toys?*
4. *What does Santa look like going down a skinny, narrow chimney?*
5. *What would Santa do if there were a fire in the fireplace at the bottom of the chimney?*
6. *When Santa gets inside the house, how will he move? Will he move quietly? On tiptoe?*
7. *How does Santa get back up the chimney?*

Snow Prints/Angels (Individuals)

Equipment: None.

For this activity the children will pretend that they are outside in the snow. Paint a vivid word picture, and to set the mood, encourage the children to do the following:

1. *Shiver in the cold.*
2. *Stomp through deep snow.*
3. *Make snowballs.*

Next, have the children lie on the floor and make an angel in the snow. You may need to demonstrate this. Break this down into parts. *Lie on your back and:*

1. *Open your legs wide and close them together.* Do several repetitions.
2. *Keep your legs closed. Start with your arms down by your side. Sweep them along the floor until your arms are touching above your head.* Do several repetitions.
3. *Start with your legs closed and your arms by your sides. As you sweep your legs open, simultaneously sweep your arms up over your head.* Do several repetitions.
4. *Move just your right (or left) arm and leg. Then move your arm and leg on the other side of your body.*

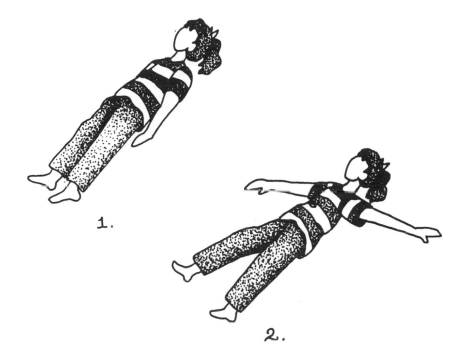

Show the children how to do the movement patterns above while standing up. Again, break the movements down first, before putting it all together. (Standing up doing an angel in the snow is the same as doing jumping jacks.)

Indoor Sledding (Groups)

Equipment: One carpet square for every two or three children; one bicycle inner tube for every two or three children.

Children can do this activity in groups of two or three, but start the activity using groups of three children. Designate one of the group to ride on the sled; the other two children will pull the sled.

Turn the carpet square upside down, so the nap is face down on the floor. The rider lies down on the sled and holds onto the inner tube. The sled pullers

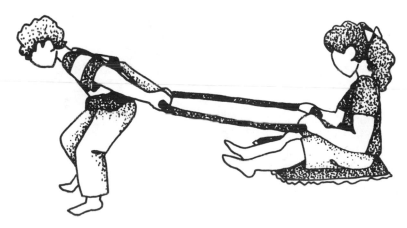

will take hold of the other end of the inner tube and pull the sled all about the room.

Demonstrate to the children the importance of not going too close to the walls. They also really need to watch out for each other. If they are running in circles, the sled may tend to make wide turns.

Work out a system for rotating riders. The rider can try sledding in various positions:

- *Lying on your tummy*
- *Lying on your back*
- *Kneeling*
- *Sitting*

The Giant Mitten (Group)

Equipment: One parachute or large blanket; the book *The Mitten* by Jan Brett, Scholastic Books, 1992.

Read the entire story of *The Mitten* to the children. Then lay the blanket flat on the floor. The blanket will be your mitten. This time as you read the story, assign one or more children to take the part of each animal. (Every child should get to participate.) They should move one time around the outside of the blanket, moving like their animal would move, and then proceed to get inside the mitten.

The teacher can take the part of the meadow mouse and wriggle into the one small space that is left inside the mitten. With the enormous sneeze, the teacher whips the blanket up and off the animals.

Variation: As the story is first read to the children, give them time to act out the movements of each character:

1. *Grandma moves slowly, bent over.*
2. *Nicki might move your favorite way of moving.*

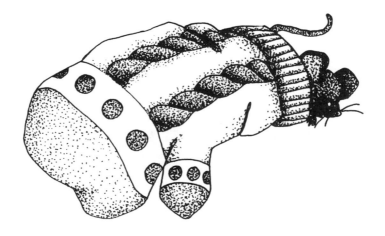

3. *Mole moves by burrowing on the ground. Try it with your eyes shut.*
4. *Rabbit moves by jumping on two feet or from hands to feet in a squatting position.*
5. *Hedgehog wiggles and waddles.*
6. *Owl moves by flying with swooping arm motions.*
7. *Badger has sharp digging claws in front.*
8. *Fox moves quickly and is a fast runner.*
9. *Bear moves slowly, lumbering.*
10. *Mouse is very small and moves quickly.*

LESSON 3

Frosty the Snowman (Warm-up)

Equipment: Record or tape of the song "Frosty The Snowman"; record or tape player.

The children will mimic the teacher's actions. The teacher faces the children for the first four stanzas. The children pretend to:

1. Hold fat belly and laugh.   *jolly, happy soul*

2. Place pipe and nose on own face.   *corncob pipe and button nose*

3. Hold hat on head and dance in place.   *magic in . . . silk hat . . . began to dance around*

4. Line up behind teacher and follow her, running, galloping, dancing, marching, and waving.   *sun was hot . . . waved good-bye*

Giant Snowballs (Groups)

Equipment: Garbage bags, preferably light colored, stuffed with newspaper and tied shut: one bag for every four children.

Each group of children forms a circle. Let the children explore with their giant snowball.

1. They can start by rolling the giant snowball to each other across the circle, then try kicking the snowball across the circle.

2. The children can try to quickly pass the snowball around the circle, either by rolling it or picking it up and passing it to each other. They can try passing it in the other direction, also. Try this with the children sitting, and then standing.

The children all sit down. Two children at a time will work together. The two should try to:

1. *Roll the snowball all about the room. Try rolling the snowball backwards and sideways, also.* Switch so the waiting children get a turn.

2. *Carry the snowball all about the room.* You may direct the movement, by suggesting forward, backward, or sideways movement.

3. Two of the group lie down on their backs. They put their legs in the air so the bottoms of their feet are pointing to the ceiling. These two children will take turns. The other two children will lift the snowball and drop it onto the feet of one of the children. This child uses his feet to push or kick the snowball up into the air. The two children lying down will alternate several turns before trading places with the two who are lifting the snowball.

4. The two children who are lying down may want to try to keep the snowball going back and forth between them, with the help of the two "lifters."

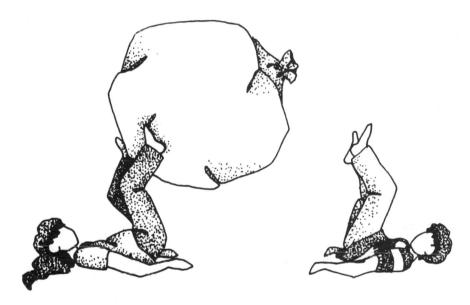

Ring Around the Snowball (Group)

Equipment: One or more garbage bag snowballs as described above.

The children form one large circle around the snowball. The children hold hands and walk around the snowball while singing the following song to the tune of "Ring Around the Rosie":

Ring around the snowball,
We're glad to see the snow fall.
Snowing, snowing
The snow falls down!

During the last two lines of the song the children stop walking, hold their hands in the air with their fingers spread and wiggling to represent falling snow. To finish the song, bring your fingers down to the floor.

Variation: Move around the circle in some manner other than walking. Each time you repeat the song, move around the circle in the opposite direction.

Avalanche! (Group)

Equipment: One garbage bag snowball as described above; one tumbling mat or other area designated as a safe area for the children.

The teacher carries the giant snowball around the room while the children move freely about the room. But the children must listen carefully, for when you yell "Avalanche!" the children must all run quickly to the designated safe area. After you yell "Avalanche!", immediately put the snowball on the floor and begin rolling it, chasing the children with the snowball.

There need be no penalty for those caught by the snowball. Just be sure that each child gets a turn being chased.

Variations:

- The teacher can dictate how the children should move before the avalanche.
- More than one snowball can be used. The children can have turns rolling the avalanche snowballs.

Indoor Snowfolk (Group)

Equipment: All of the garbage bag snowballs used in this lesson; black and orange construction paper; masking tape.

Use masking tape to hold the snowballs together as you stack them up to make snowpeople. Use two or three snowballs for each snowperson. Cut eye and mouth pieces out of the black construction paper; cut a "carrot" nose out of the orange construction paper. Use the masking tape to tape the faces onto the snowfolk.

LESSON 4

Down the Hill, Up the Hill (Warm-up)

Equipment: Tumbling mats.

Each child finds space on the tumbling mats.

1. *Today we are all going sledding. Sit on your sled and hold on to the rope. Here we go down the hill! When you get to the bottom of the hill, roll off your sled.*

2. *Now get up and pull your sled up the hill. (Stay in your own space and walk in place.) This time let's lie on our tummies. Put your feet up. Here we go! Remember to roll off the sled at the bottom of the hill.*

3. *Let's pull the sled back up the hill. This time let's lie on our backs. Hold on to the rope. Roll off at the bottom. And here we go back up the hill.*

4. *Let's ride on our knees this time. We're going down the biggest hill ever. Lean way over to the side. Don't fall off. Lean to the other side. Hold on! Lean back the other way. Now the other way. Watch for the bump at the bottom! Remember to roll off the sled. Pull your sled back up the hill.*

Variation: This is also great fun if all of the children sit in a line one behind the other, with their legs wrapped around each other as if they were on one giant toboggan. *Lean to the left, to the right, lean back, and lean forward. And sometimes you all roll off!*

Partner Snow Prints (Partners)

Equipment: None.

The children need partners. Before doing this activity the children need to be familiar with the Snow Prints (Angels) activity in Lesson 2. Review with the children how to do the snow prints while standing up. Decide which of the partners will be the first leader. The partners stand facing one another and the leader moves just one arm, or an arm and a leg, or both arms, as if doing a standing snow angel. His partner copies his movements as if she were looking in a mirror. The partners can take several turns being the leader.

Stay in the Barn! (Group)

Equipment: One tumbling mat, or boundary markers to mark off a "safe" area for the children.

Use the tumbling mat or the boundary markers to mark off a space which represents the barn. You assume the role of Santa, and tell the reindeer (all of the children) to stay in the nice warm barn and rest so they'll have lots of energy for pulling the sleigh on Christmas Eve. "Santa" then walks to the other side of the room and goes to work in his toy shop. While his back is turned, the reindeer sneak out of the barn and walk quietly up behind Santa. When Santa discovers what the reindeer have done, he yells "The reindeer are out! The reindeer are out!" and chases them back to the barn. Any reindeer caught become elves who help Santa.

Embellish the game by having one or more elves go through the process of closing the barn door, locking the door, pounding nails in the door, or anything else you can think of to keep the reindeer inside.

The Gingerbread Boy

Equipment: A copy of the story "The Gingerbread Boy."

The children sit in a circle and you begin reading the story of the gingerbread boy. When you get to the part about the gingerbread boy being chased by the little old man and the little old woman, encourage the children to chase you about the room. When you come back to the circle and sit down, that is the signal for the children to do the same so the story can continue. Each time a different

animal or person in the story chases the gingerbread boy, the children likewise chase you.

At the end of the story, everyone should be a fox. Swim by lying on the floor. Challenge the children to really "see" the gingerbread boy as he moves from the fox's tail, to her back, up to her shoulder, and then on her nose.

Variation: The children could act out the story in another manner. They can be challenged to move the way the different characters (or "chasers") in the story might move. How would the old man and old woman move? How would the cow move? Or the horse? What about the workers in the field?

Valentine's Day

LESSON 1

Heart to Heart (Individuals)

Equipment: At least one 1½-inch to 3-inch construction paper heart per child; masking tape; a triangle, drum or other musical instrument for cuing the children.

Tape the hearts to the walls and the floor all about the room. Tape the hearts at various heights on the walls, but keep all of the hearts within reach of the children.

The children move freely about the room. When the teacher taps the triangle, the children run quickly to any of the hearts and touch the heart.

You may want to designate how the children should move. You may also indicate with which body part the children should touch the hearts. It is easier for the children if you wait until they are standing by the hearts before telling them which body part to use.

To make the game more of a memory or concentration game, tell the children which body part to use *before* they start moving in the room. Then, when the (triangle) signal is given, let the children go to a heart and place the correct body part on it without reminding them what part to use. Point out those children who have remembered correctly, and the others will automatically and inconspicuously correct themselves.

Variation: Give each child one of the hearts with a masking tape loop on the back of it. The children stick the valentines to the body part named and proceed to move about the room in the manner indicated. When the sound cue is given, the children each find partners and stand with their paper hearts touching. For example, if they tape the hearts to their elbows, when the signal is given, each person finds a partner and they stand elbow to elbow. Instead of a musical instrument, the stop signal can be you saying "Heart to Heart!"

Wake Up, Cupid (Group)

Equipment: One to four large grocery sacks, shoe boxes, or other containers; at least one valentine or construction paper heart per child.

The children line up side by side at one end of the room. Designate one child as Cupid. Cupid stands at the other end of the room with her back turned to the others. She closes her eyes and pretends to be sleeping. The containers are placed behind Cupid.

The children go together as a group, trying to sneak up behind Cupid to place their valentines in one of the containers. Warn the children, however, that if Cupid wakes up, she will chase them back to their starting line. If Cupid tags anyone, they have to become Cupid's helpers and help to tag the others. Continue the game until everyone is a Cupid's helper.

It is important that the children go together as a group to deliver their valentines to Cupid. There will be too many collisions if some children are sneaking up on Cupid while others are running away from her.

Hand out the original valentines (or different ones) each time the children take a turn sneaking up on Cupid.

Variation: Cupid has to stay asleep and cannot chase anyone until the children yell "Wake Up, Cupid!"

Cupid's Heart (Group)

Equipment: Masking tape or gym tape (or spot markers).

Use the tape or the spot markers to make a giant heart shape on the floor in the middle of the room. The heart has to be big enough for all of the children to fit inside when they are standing.

Cupid lives inside the heart. You can be Cupid, or you can designate one of the children to be Cupid. The other children gather around the outside of the heart. If the children dare to step inside the heart, then Cupid may tag them. Anyone tagged by Cupid must join Cupid inside the heart and become a "tagger." Play the game until everyone has been tagged, or until you can no longer coax the children to step inside the heart.

Some children are more daring than others. There are children who will resist getting too close to the heart or stepping inside it at all. Play the game within the children's comfort zones. It isn't necessarily important that all of the children be tagged.

Coach the children to say something pleasant to Cupid when they step inside the heart. (Immediately eliminate any taunting.) The children might say, "Happy Valentine's Day!" when they step near or inside the heart.

Variation: Cupid can touch anyone who is inside or outside the heart, but Cupid must always stay inside the heart. So even if children are standing outside the heart, but are very close to it, they are vulnerable to being tagged.

Special Delivery (Group)

Equipment: Four paper sacks (lunch size or larger) for each group; four valentines or construction paper hearts for each group.

Divide the class into three to five groups. To eliminate a lot of waiting time, try to have no more than four children in each group. Each group lines up one behind the other at one end of the room.

Place four sacks in a row (3 feet apart) in front of each group. The first person in each group has four valentines. On the "go" signal, he runs to the first bag and drops in one valentine; he runs to the second bag and drops in the second valentine. He continues in this manner until he has delivered all of his valentines, at which point he returns to his group.

When all of the first runners have finished, the valentines are collected so the second runner can have her turn (unless each runner starts with four valentines or paper hearts).

LESSON 2

Heart Shapes (Individuals and Partners)

Equipment: Drawings or cutouts of heart shapes; any lively music; tape or record player.

Show the children the heart-shaped drawings. Challenge the children to make heart shapes with their arms and then with their legs.

1. *Is there any other way you can make a heart shape with your body? Try making heart shapes while standing and also while lying down.*
2. Challenge the children to make a heart shape with a partner. Some children will try making a heart while lying down, and others will do so while standing. Point this out to the group so the children try it both ways.
3. Ask the children if they can keep this heart shape with a partner while moving in the room.
4. Partners should separate and move about the room while music plays. When the music stops, children should quickly find a new partner and make a heart shape. The children should move individually about the room. Challenge them to move in various directions or using different locomotor skills.

Valentine's Day (Group)

Equipment: Chalk, tape, or space markers to mark two lines at opposite ends of the room.

The children stand side by side on a line at one end of the room. Designate another line across the room to which the children should run. You stand in the middle of the room between the two lines.

The children ask you, "What day is it?" You answer by naming a day of the week or a holiday, such as Halloween, Christmas, or Thanksgiving. The children keep asking you "What day is it?" until you answer, "It's Valentine's Day!" That's the signal for the children to run to the other end of the room. You try to tag the children as they are running.

Any child who is tagged must join you in the middle of the room. Now, to avoid confusion, you should cue your helpers as to how to answer to "What day is it?" so they are all giving the same answer. Be sure to discuss with the children how to safely chase and tag.

Be My Valentine (Group)

Equipment: A package of valentines that has at least two or three copies of each particular valentine. Hand out a valentine to each child, making sure that you have given its duplicate to at least one other child; music source.

While lively music is playing, the children move about the room. When the music stops, the children should find the person(s) who has the valentine that matches their own. When they find the match, they say to each other, "Be My Valentine!" and sit down together.

Before the music starts again, the children should trade with each other so they have a different valentine. When the music stops, find the person whose valentine matches the new design.

Remember that you can also indicate how the children should move in the room: backwards, sideways, galloping, tiptoeing, marching, etc.

Heart, Heart, Valentine (Group)

Equipment: One valentine.

The children sit in a circle. One person, designated as Cupid, walks around the outside of the circle holding a valentine. As he walks around the circle, he taps each person on the head; as he does so he says "Heart" with each tap. At some point Cupid will lay the valentine on the floor behind one of the children and say, "Valentine." This child jumps up and chases Cupid around the circle back to the spot where the valentine is lying on the floor.

The advantage of using a valentine is that it marks the spot to where the children should run. If the designated "Valentine" catches Cupid, Cupid has to sit in the middle of the circle for one turn. Otherwise Cupid takes Valentine's spot on the circle, and it is Valentine's turn to be Cupid.

It is important to play this game until every child has had at least one turn to run. The children might give a signal, such as sitting with their thumbs up, if they have not had a turn to be the Valentine. Then the Cupid knows to look for someone with their thumbs up to choose as a Valentine.

Easter

LESSON 1

Egg Roll (Individuals)

Equipment: One plastic egg or dyed tennis ball per child.

The children will find different ways to roll the eggs on the floor. For example, challenge the children to place the egg carefully on the floor, then roll the egg along the floor using their noses. Encourage the children to use other body parts to roll the eggs, such as elbows, thumbs, knees, toes, and so on.

> **Variation:**   The children can find partners, and the partners can try rolling the eggs back and forth to each other. They also can try using various body parts to do the rolling.

Bunny Hop (Individuals)

Equipment: Tape or record of the song "The Bunny Hop;" tape or record player.

This can be done as an individual activity first, so the children become familiar with the steps.

Stand with your hands on your hips. Touch out (to the front and side) with one foot. Touch with your heel only, toe pointing up. (Some will be able to do this; others will not.) *Do two touches on one side, bounce your knees, and then do two touches with your other foot. Follow this by jumping forward three jumps.* Start over from the beginning using the touch step.

> **Variation:**   When the children are first learning the dance, they may want to do just one touch step on each side and bounce their knees in between. The younger the child, the slower the reaction time. Allowing them to do only one touch step on each side may allow them to keep in step with the jumps. Experiment to see which method allows the children to have the most success.

You may also vary the dance by designating which way the children should jump: forward, backwards, or sideways. Do several repetitions of each direction so the children do not become too confused.

Bunny Hop Conga Line (Group)

Equipment: Tape or record of the song "The Bunny Hop;" tape or record player.

It may be easier to have the children first learn the steps individually as described above. Then line the children up one behind the other. Each child puts his hands on the shoulders of the person in front of her. Emphasize to the children that they should only lightly touch the shoulders of the front person.

When the children are first learning the dance, it may be easier to have smaller groups, such as four or five people. Then progress to two groups together, and so on, until the whole class is in one long line.

Proceed with the dance steps as listed in "Bunny Hop," the preceding activity.

Easter Egg Hunt (Group)

Equipment:　As many plastic eggs or dyed tennis balls as possible.

Divide the class into two groups. One group of children will start the game by being the "Hiders," and one group will start the game as the "Hunters." It will be the responsibility of the Hiders to hide all of the eggs all over the room (with teacher limitations, if needed), while the Hunters either leave the room with another teacher or hide their eyes.

Divide the eggs evenly among the Hiders before they start hiding the eggs. Emphasize to the Hunters just exactly how many eggs each of them is to find before coming back to the group and sitting down.

If each child will be carrying a large number of eggs, the children may need plastic egg "buckets." Then the Hiders can share with the Hunters.

Not all of the balls have to be completely hidden. It is okay to leave some in the corners of the room, and others only partially hidden. The Hiders and the Hunters keep alternating turns until the children tire of the game (or until they have to go home).

Spoon Carry (Group)

Equipment: Four tablespoons; four plastic buckets; one egg per child; spot markers or a line at one end of the room.

Divide the class into four groups. Each group lines up one behind the other at one end of the room. Across the room, 10 feet to 15 feet in front of each group, are the plastic buckets.

Each child stands in line holding his egg. The front person in each group is given a spoon, into which he places his egg. When the signal is given, each leader is to carry his egg (in his spoon) across the room to his bucket. When he reaches the bucket, he drops his egg into the bucket and walks back to his group.

The next person in line then takes his turn to carry his egg to the bucket. The first person waits at the end of his own line.

Variation: After each child carries his egg to the bucket, the game is played again. This time each child must carry an empty spoon to the bucket, scoop up one egg, and balance it on his spoon as he walks back to his group.

Safety Note: It is very important that the children not run with the empty spoon. If there is a real propensity to run, then give each child a spoon, and they can drop the spoon into the bucket along with their egg. Then they run back to their group empty-handed.

Egg Gathering (Group)

Equipment: Sixteen plastic eggs or dyed tennis balls; sixteen spot markers; four plastic bucket Easter baskets; a line at one end of the room.

The class is divided into four groups. Each group lines up one behind the other behind the starting line. In front of each group are four spot markers placed one in front of the other about 3 feet apart from each other. On top of each spot marker is an egg.

The front person in each group runs with the Easter basket to collect her four Easter eggs. She then runs back to her group with her basket of eggs. After each front person returns with her basket of eggs, you instruct her to place the eggs back on the spots so the next person can have a turn. Play the game until each person has had a turn to collect the Easter eggs.

Variation: The game can be played continuously if the first person collects the eggs, the second person places the eggs back on the spots, the third person collects the eggs, and so on.

It's Easter! (Group)

Equipment: Two lines, one at each end of the room.

This is a variation of the game "It's Valentine's Day!" For this game, however, the children run when you announce "It's Easter!"

Summer

LESSON 1

Swimming (Warm-up)

Equipment: Tumblings mats are optional.

Tumbling mats will make it easier for the children to visualize the "water." First, the children should gather around the water. Point out that the water is very chilly.

1. *Step very carefully into the water; just dip one foot in. Is it cold? Does it make you shiver? Now quickly put the other foot in; then run and splash in the water.*
2. *Now let's lie down and swim. Don't forget to kick your legs, too.*
3. *Can you turn over on your back and do the back stroke?*
4. *Let's rest by just floating on our backs for a bit.*
5. *Can you swim when you are lying on your side?*

Variation: The children can do the swimming strokes while walking or running in the room. *Do the front crawl by moving forward, the back crawl while moving backwards, and the side stroke while moving sideways.*

Use this opportunity to talk with the children about safety near water. Especially emphasize the idea of not wading or swimming unless an adult is present.

Fishing (Individuals)

Equipment: None. (Ribbons are optional.)

The children pretend to go fishing. (If using the ribbons, they are the fishing pole and fishing line all in one.) Show the children how to cast the line and then reel it in. Encourage the children to try casting with the other hand, too.

After the children have practiced casting for some time, point out that they have now caught a giant fish—as big as a shark. Encourage them to really hold on to the fishing pole: *Don't let go. Pull back. Hold on and walk back slowly. Keep reeling slowly. Does the fish break the line and swim away, or did you catch it?*

Upside Down Bicycling (Individuals)

Equipment: None.

We're now going to get out our bicycles and go for a ride. But these bikes are

254

special. These are upside down bicycles. You ride them by lying down on your back, putting your feet in the air, and pedaling. Pedal as fast as you can! Can anyone pedal backwards?

Human Croquet (Group)

Equipment: One tennis ball for every two children.

Divide the class into two groups. One group will be standing in a random formation all about the room. These children are the croquet wickets, and they stand with their feet at least shoulder-width apart.

The partners each have a tennis ball. They move about the room trying to roll their tennis ball through each wicket. The wickets should be cautioned to stand very still. Encourage the children to find unique ways to roll the tennis balls, such as backwards through their own legs, or while sitting down and rolling it under their own bent knees.

Let the children trade jobs at least one or two times.

Preschool Hopscotch (Group)

Equipment: Non-skid spot markers or carpet squares.

Lay out a variety of simple hopscotch patterns using non-skid spot markers or carpet squares. Try to have several hopscotch patterns so the children do not need to wait in line a long time. Demonstrate each pattern for the children.

This really is an exercise in discriminating between a hop and a jump. Wherever there is just one marker, the children will hop. Where there are two markers side by side, the children will jump. Be sure to let the children practice hopping and jumping before they try the hopscotch.

Use your imagination in setting up the patterns. Simply vary the number and sequence of hops and jumps.

Variations:

1. Instead of jumping and hopping, the children can clap. Two spots side by side would indicate two claps. A solo spot would require one clap, as the children walk through the pattern.

2. For four- and five-year-olds, try using color variations to indicate the movement pattern. For example, use two colors of spots, say yellow and orange. Lay the spots down in single file, varying the yellow and orange. The yellow could indicate jumping, and the orange would be hopping.

Shark! (Group)

Equipment: Mark two lines, one at each end of the room.

1. The children all stand on the line at one end of the room. The children are all fish now, and point out that they will be swimming back and forth across the room. The line they are now on is the ship. When the teacher gives the signal, they should all swim to the other line, which is the shore. Practice the swimming and the signals a few times. You may say, "Swim to the ship," or "Swim to the shore." Before the children reach the other side of the room (the ship), you may tell them "Swim to the shore," so they have to turn around right where they are and swim to the shore. Quick and frequent changes of direction makes this game fun.

2. Next point out that waiting on the sidelines is a very dangerous shark (you). When you shout, "Shark!" the fish are in danger of being eaten by the shark. The shark will then come running and try to tag the children. The only way the fish can be safe is to lie down flat on the floor and touch at least one other person. This is different than most tag games, in that the children are not safe by running to the other line. Emphasize that they need to lie down right where they are—even in the middle of the ocean. Then they are safe as long as they are reaching out and touching

at least one other fish. The children will need to practice this several times before beginning the game. The tendency will be for the children to run to the other line as soon as they hear "Shark!"

3. Any of the fish tagged by the Shark will then join the Shark in tagging the other fish. Continue until every fish has been caught.

Variation: Add other signals so the fish need to respond differently to the various signals. For example, if you say "*Whale!*," the children will need to stop and hop on one foot in order to be safe. (They also may have to be touching another person.) If you say "*Turtle!*" the children need to lie on their backs with their feet in the air.

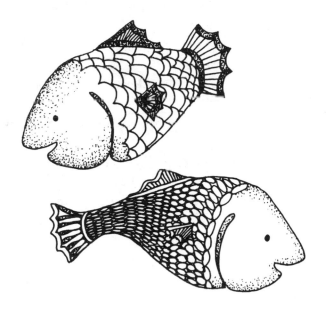

Bibliography

Brehm, Madeleine and Tindell, Nancy T. *Movement With a Purpose*. West Nyack, New York: Parker Publishing Company, Inc., 1983.

Gilliom, Bonnie Cherp. *Basic Movement Education for Children: Rationale and Teaching Units*. Reading, Massachusetts: Addison-Wesley Publishing Company, 1970.

Harris, Jane A., Anne Pittman, and Marlys S. Waller. *Dance a While*. Minneapolis: Burgess Publishing Company, 1964.

Horne, Virginia Lee. *Stunts and Tumbling for Girls*. New York: The Ronald Press Company, 1943.

Johnson, Laura. *Simplified Rhythm Stick Activities*. Long Branch, New Jersey: Kimbo Educational 07740, 1976.

Kirchner, Glenn. *Physical Education for Elementary School Children*. Dubuque, Iowa: Wm. C. Brown Company, 1970.

Orlick, Terry. *The Cooperative Sports and Games Book*. New York: Pantheon Books, 1978.

Stewart, Georgiana. *A Thriller for Kids*. Long Branch, New Jersey: Kimbo Educational Records, 1984.

Sobel, Jeffrey. *Everybody Wins*. New York: Walker and Company, 1983.

Wild, Monica R. and Doris E. White. *Physical Education for Elementary Schools*. Cedar Falls, Iowa: University of Northern Iowa, 1966.

Wilson, Meredith. *Chicken Fat*. Long Branch, New Jersey: Kimbo Educational.

Physical Activities for the Mentally Retarded. Washington, D.C.: AAHPERD Publications, 1968.

Disney Pardners. Burbank, California: Disneyland/Vista Records, 1980.

Index